On the Counselor's Path

A GUIDE TO TEACHING
BRIEF SOLUTION-FOCUSED THERAPY

A. J. Chevalier, Ph.D.

NEW HARBINGER PUBLICATIONS, INC.

Publisher's Note

This publication is designed to provide accurate and authoritative information in regard to the subject matter covered. It is sold with the understanding that the publisher is not engaged in rendering psychological, financial, legal, or other professional services. If expert assistance or counseling is needed, the services of a competent professional should be sought.

Copyright © 1996 A. J. Chevalier
New Harbinger Publications, Inc.
5674 Shattuck Avenue
Oakland, CA 94609

Cover design by SHELBY DESIGNS & ILLUSTRATES.
Text design by Tracy Marie Powell.

Distributed in the U.S.A. primarily by Publishers Group West; in Canada by Raincoast Books; in Great Britain by Airlift Book Company, Ltd.; in South Africa by Real Books, Ltd.; in Australia by Boobook; and in New Zealand by Tandem Press.

ISBN 1-57224-048-2

First printing 1996, 500 copies.

Every question is an opening
to new understanding.
Let us honor each other
where we are
and
wait patiently
for
more light.

Contents

Acknowledgments

I wish to thank Farrin Jacobs for her diligent editorial review of this manuscript, the support of Kirk Johnson and the staff of New Harbinger, and these clinical supervisors: Robert Becker, Bud Protinsky, Mike Sporakowski, Jim Keller, Steve Elliott, Joyce Simon-Lantor, and Insoo Berg.

Introduction

Using This Guidebook

The guidebook is offered to workshop leaders, practicum instructors, students, veteran clinicians, and clinical supervisors as a training tool. Its purpose is to guide the teaching, learning, and practicing of Brief Solution-Focused Therapy. Instructors, students, and workshop leaders will find it helpful to use the exercises here in conjunction with *On the Clients Path: A Manual for the Practice of Solution-Focused Therapy*. Each chapter in the manual corresponds to the same numbered chapter in the guidebook. Each chapter in the Guidebook brings solution-focused concepts to life through the experience and fun of exercises. Chapters can be done one at a time, allowing participants to absorb the concepts and ask good questions. Any participant in a given group can lead these exercises.

Each exercise is described in terms of length of time needed, materials needed, concepts, steps to take, issues to discuss, and questions to consider. Common scenarios that therapists encounter follow each of the exercises. Solution-focused techniques are applied to such situations as taking stock of counseling skills, working with persons of different lifestyles, easing conflict with peers, and accepting personal differences.

All of the exercises are starting points. What is thrilling is where group questions *take* the learning. If it is possible for the leader to demonstrate a therapy session for the whole group, that would prove to be an added benefit; however, this is not a requirement.

The purposes of *On the Client's Path* and the guidebook are simple. There seems to be quite a bit of mystery and excitement about Solution-Focused Therapy these days. It generates a good deal of attention. Many clinicians say they are mystified by it. I believe that remaining mystified or in awe of something means that we cannot master it. If we cannot master it, then it must be magic. The first purpose of the Guidebook and the Manual is to *remove the mystery*—to move from magic to method.

The second purpose, while connected to the first one, is more altruistic. If there is less mystery about how to do this kind of therapy, then more therapists can use it and quite simply *more clients can be helped.* In addition, clinical supervisors and their trainees can work together to uncover their own strengths and enjoy doing it at the same time.

Philosophy of the Guidebook

The Philosophy in this book of exercises can be summarized as follows:

> "Everyone is a student and everyone is a teacher. It is more than possible to bring different levels of expertise together; it is an exciting chance of growth for all present at the time."

When I work as a group leader with therapists as they work with clients:

- I find something good in what they are already doing.

  They find that hard to resist.

- I ask them to list their strengths and skills.

  They find that a challenge that leaves them feeling good.

- I find a strength in each piece of work they present.

  They pay close attention to what I am saying.

- I call "weaknesses" challenges. This encourages all.

  They discover the work they need to do.

- I respond to a question first with a compliment and then by considering it seriously.

  This creates an atmosphere where questions are thrilling.

- I listen for the therapists' view of things and use it to help them.

  They listen incredibly well to their own views.

- I honor confusion and enlist its support as the "beginning of clarity."

  Confused persons drop their fear and begin to learn.

- I honor therapists' experiences.

  They become very willing to share their experiences.

- I recognize the richness of difference in therapists and ask that they do the same.

  Respecting difference opens all our eyes and ears.

- I weave therapists' responses into a group experience or discussion.

  Everyone feels they have a part in the group.

- What concerns the therapists concerns me.

  Everyone feels they are legitimate learners.

- I trust them to chart their paths of learning.

  This frees us all to learn in our own ways and to offer unique contributions to the group.

Then there are exceptions:

- If I find a therapist irritating, I ask myself, "What is this person showing me about me?"

- I see a therapist's behavior as behavior and not the therapist.

- If a person likes to argue, I look for the positives in the expression.

- I make sure that I understand the view of each participant.

- I see others inspiring me: We are all great teachers.

- I find a way to honor each exchange I have with others.

- Together we honor what each client brings.

Remove the mystery.
More therapists can be trained.
More people may be helped.
And training can be an enlightening process.
The wisdom of all may just rise to the top.
Such a collective wisdom blesses all, forgets none.
What a world that would be!

A.J. Chevalier, Ph.D.
El Rito, New Mexico

1

About Wisdom, Honor, and Respect

In Chapter 1, we learn the purpose of respect and honor for each client who comes for help. The first two exercises start the therapists on this journey. Before they can begin learning the skills necessary to understand the client, they must first practice opening themselves up to this knowledge. The third exercise takes stock of current counseling skills, offering each therapist a place to start.

Exercise 1: Myself in Metaphor

This exercise takes the therapist out of the usual ways of thinking about self and others in order to learn to withhold judgment while visiting a client's world. For example, if one can think about the self as a turtle or gardener, then one can think about the steps needed to take to develop as a turtle or gardener. This development is seen through the symbol of the turtle or the gardener so there is far less chance for harsh judgment of the self. Also, it is fun to think of the self in ways not previously tried. This development can be playfully traced for years, a semester, or the duration of a conference or workshop.

Time: Explanation - 15 minutes
Assignment - length of time in workshop or length of semester

Materials: None

Concept: Understanding the stage of my development as a therapist through a metaphor

Directions

1. Explain "metaphor" using a dictionary definition.

2. Ask participants to select a metaphor that fits them as developing therapists. Allow group members time to think about their choices.

3. Ask each member to give a reason for her/his choice.

4. Assign a 1–5 page paper written in first person about their development as a therapist over the course of the workshop/semester. The paper should be written at the end of the workshop/semester and should trace the member's development as a therapist in the language of the metaphor over the course of the workshop/semester.

Issues for Discussion

- Benefits of looking at oneself from a metaphorical position

- Benefits of group discussion about the metaphorical stances

Questions to Consider

1. What does my metaphor say to me about my strengths as a therapist?

2. What does my metaphor say about my current challenges as a therapist?

3. As my metaphor, what goals do I need to achieve?

4. For myself, can I list these goals? (State in measurable terms)

Participant Affirmation

I am all I need right now to achieve the goals I set for myself.

Leader Affirmation

I can reach a new understanding of myself and I can lead this group to new understandings of themselves.

Vignette 1

Goal: Promote growth in group members by using SFT principles and images

Example: In listening to group participants talk, I became aware of one person's need to understand all concepts in clinical terms or in intellectual ideas. Steps were all logical and methodical and there was no room for looking at clinical ideas in alternate ways. This group member took great pride in how she "understood" therapy and described strategies and interventions. She refused to "see" herself any other way.

Challenge: The challenge is to view this person's intellectual understanding and conceptual knowledge as vital for her, honor her way, and resist asking her to change. In her current perspective, using SFT principles, this person can be invited to see things in a new and exciting way.

Intervention: As the leader, I acknowledged a strength in every group member out loud. That was followed by asking each member to select a symbol that stood for their growth and development thus far as a therapist. I left her to almost last so that she would build anticipation for her compliment. Doing this helped her to listen carefully for a compliment that fit her. Here is that strategy: "I am impressed with your ways of discussing ideas and concepts. I invite you to use these ways as you select an image for your own growth up to this moment." With this compliment and gentle group pressure she complied with the group task.

SFT Principle: Accept the client view and use compliments that fit. Expect growth and change.

Exercise 2: When I Was Honored

This exercise looks at how it feels to be honored and gets the therapist in touch with how this feels. Once the therapist can feel this again, there is a greater chance that this atmosphere can be offered to clients. Honoring the client means respecting the client and the client's world. This is a practice, a set of behaviors that forms basic habits for doing therapy.

Time: 30–45 minutes

Materials: Chalk, board

Concept: Studying how it feels to be honored

Directions

1. Ask members to relax and close their eyes.

2. Ask them to recall a time when they felt that others honored them.

3. Ask them to see the faces around them at that time.

4. Ask them to remember how they felt.

5. Ask them to remember what the others did that let them know they were being honored.

6. Ask members to stay there until they are ready to come back to the room where they are sitting.

7. Allow about 5 minutes before asking members to come back to the room.

8. Spend the next 15 minutes discussing the feelings they had. Make a list of these feelings on the board.

9. Ask members to consider the benefits of therapy to clients when honor is part of the therapy.

Issues for Discussion

- Therapy experiences members have had and whether they felt honored

- What their therapists did that honored or dishonored them
- The effects of honor or dishonor on the therapy experience

Questions to Consider

1. What impact would a context full of honor (as you have just experienced) have on clients? On therapy?

2. What skills do you have that would promote an honoring context?

3. What traits do you need to develop to promote an honoring context?

Participant Affirmation

I define the steps in my learning process.

Leader Affirmation

I trust group members to define their paths of learning.

Vignette 2

Goal: To look at the feelings that are in the experience of being honored

Example: One group member had extreme difficulty with accepting compliments, even when the ones selected obviously fit. Her discomfort was recognized by group members, some of whom commented on her body language when she was complimented. Some wanted her to accept the compliments readily, but she hesitated repeatedly.

Challenge: To honor an individual's stance when others are pulling on her to be different and more like them. The challenge is to honor her *and* them.

Intervention: As the group leader, I made eye contact with each member after this exchange and said these words: "It is interesting to see that others have all kinds of different responses. This gives me a real chance to learn how other people see things. I also get the chance to try to honor someone else's view, without rearranging it."

SFT Principle: Seeing and respecting all the views I am offered by others.

Exercise 3: My Strengths and Challenges—Setting My Goals

This exercise sets in motion an assessment of current counseling skills and the steps each therapist needs to take to improve. Essentially, each therapist is charting his/her own path, setting goals and watching for improvement.

Time: 1 hour for verbal behaviors and 1 hour for nonverbal behaviors

Materials: Barbara Okun's counseling skills list (found on page 7 in the manual)

Concept: Assessing my counseling skills

Directions

1. Ask participants to list verbal behaviors of a good counselor. Ask them to rank these in order of importance.

2. Ask members to write a statement of relationship between counselor behaviors that are important and goals they have for themselves as counselors.

3. Repeat #1 and #2 with nonverbal behaviors that members consider good for a therapist to do.

4. Compare with Okun's list from the manual.

5. Ask members to write a list of three verbal and three nonverbal behaviors that can be goals for themselves.

6. Ask members to put these goals in measurable form, for example, "I will listen better," becomes "I will interrupt no more than three times in my next session with a client".

7. Goals may be posted for each group member if each is agreeable to this.

Issues for Discussion

- Setting realistic goals
- Putting goals in measurable form
- Asking members to watch for and compliment signs of progress in one another

Questions to Consider

1. What does asking for help mean to you?
2. What does accepting help mean to you?
3. What does being in therapy mean to you?
4. What does it mean to be developing as a therapist?

Participant Affirmation

I can grow by asking for and accepting help from others.

Leader Affirmation

I believe the group has its own power to teach us what we need to learn.

Vignette 3

Goal: To help group members listen for and remember compliments that fit other members' views of themselves

Example: Asking group members to take stock of their counseling skills seems like an easy task. However, many group members found this difficult to do, especially when asked to do so aloud in the group. Discussing how each member felt about assessing their skills proved to be challenging as well.

Challenge: Understanding what I do well and what others do well, and how each of us feels about that.

Intervention: Making eye contact with each member of the group, I said these words: "It is good for us to understand our personal responses to compliments. When we understand and accept what we do well, that helps us to sift out what our next goals for growth will be."

SFT Principle: Accepting persons where they are and finding strengths in them. Also setting up the best condition for the best listening the group can do by using compliments.

SKILLSHEET 1 Basic Counseling Skills—Exercise 3

Instruction: This skillsheet may be handed out to participants at the beginning of this group session.

	Not Evident	Needs Work	Good	Very Good
1. Greets client in reassuring manner	1	2	3	4
2. Explains client rights	1	2	3	4
3. Explains counselor role	1	2	3	4
4. Explains confidentiality	1	2	3	4
5. Explains structure of session (video, length)	1	2	3	4
6. Answers client questions	1	2	3	4
7. Seating at optimal distance/position	1	2	3	4
8. Eye contact matches client's behavior	1	2	3	4
9. Counselor's facial behavior shows interest, attention	1	2	3	4
10. Counselor in relaxed position	1	2	3	4

	Not Evident	Needs Work	Good	Very Good
11. Counselor varies vocal tone and pitch to show interest and attention	1	2	3	4
12. Use of one-word affirmations—"hmm," "yes"	1	2	3	4
13. Counselor uses client language	1	2	3	4
14. Counselor leans forward to show interest	1	2	3	4
15. Counselor appears aware of own body language	1	2	3	4
16. Use of open-ended questions	1	2	3	4
17. Use of clarification	1	2	3	4
18. Use of reflection	1	2	3	4
19. Counselor pursues client topic	1	2	3	4
20. Counselor helps client form specific goals	1	2	3	4
21. Counselor restates goals	1	2	3	4
22. Counselor uses more questions than interpretations	1	2	3	4
23. Counselor allows silence when needed	1	2	3	4
24. Counselor interrupts when needed	1	2	3	4
25. Counselor behavior shows comfort with client affect	1	2	3	4
26. Counselor uses summary skills	1	2	3	4
27. Appropriate ending of session	1	2	3	4
28. Sets next appointment	1	2	3	4
29. Collects fee	1	2	3	4
30. Make notes in file	1	2	3	4

2

Premises of Solution-Focused Therapy

In Chapter 2, we examine the theoretical basis for SFT. We take in the idea that an event can mean many things to its participants, and acute listening is required on the part of the therapist in order to decipher these meanings. We move past the destructive power of mistakes, using these moments as lessons.

Exercise 1: What It Means to Me

This exercise shows all the members of the group how multiple meanings can occur from the same event. This puts into practice listening skills that hear the nuance of meaning from each person.

Time: 30 minutes

Materials: Chalk, board

Concept: Finding multiple meanings of the same event

Directions

1. Ask members to recall a particular personal loss. Each member chooses their own issue to discuss.

2. Ask each to describe what this meant to them in one or two sentences.

3. Instruct members to listen for all the various meanings given to this event by group members.

4. Have them characterize in a phrase what this loss meant to each group member.

5. Put these descriptions on a number line on the board; the number line shows the continuum of feelings under the heading of "loss." Discuss how closely related these meanings are or are not.

Issues for Discussion

- Value of personal meanings in life events

- What "difference" means to the group

- How group members would like their opinions to be treated

Questions to Consider

1. How do you know someone really understands the meaning you give to an event in your life?

2. How do you know someone trusts the way you see something?

3. What is the effect on you when others understand you and trust the meanings you give to the events in your life?

Participant Affirmation

My personal meanings are important to me, I let others have their own meanings.

Leader Affirmation

I make my own meaning out of any event. There are those who will agree and those who will disagree. I accept that others have their own opinions.

Vignette 1

Goal: Addressing the idea of a lifestyle different than my own

Example: In our group, members were struggling with the idea of serving persons with different lifestyles than their own, such as different sexual preferences and orientation, persons with fewer resources so that childrearing was vastly different, etc.

Challenge: In applying SFT principles, the leader wants to keep the focus on accepting and honoring differences. The leader wants to refuse to argue about "normal lifestyles" or the "right way." The premise here is that accepting differences leads to cooperation and honoring differences leads to personal growth and personal power.

Intervention: As the group leader, I refused gently an invitation that asked me to pass judgment on people different than me. I used these words: "You know, I have found that when I preach to people, they rarely listen. When I ask, beg, and try to force them to change, they rarely do. I got tired of trying. What *I can do*, is find out what each person wants from therapy and help them achieve that goal. If I feel I cannot serve a particular group of people, then that is my issue and must be looked at in relation to the Code of Ethics and my personal code of conduct as a therapist and human. Sometimes that means that I have a problem that needs work. I take that to an appropriate person and we work it out—outside the therapy hour. I watch for this issue to rear its head though in the next therapy hours, as clients inevitably touch on my own issues."

SFT Principle: Looking at forcing meaning upon others, going with what clients present and working with my own issues on my own time

Exercise 2: Mistakes

This exercise tells us something about what it is like to make a mistake, that is, how each group member approaches mistakes. Group members can also look at being wrong and what that means to each of them. Attitudes and feelings can be discussed and a new attitude or new feelings toward mistakes can be derived from discussion.

Time: 30 minutes

Materials: None

Concept: Discovering the meanings we give to our mistakes

Directions

1. Ask each member to take part in word association beginning with the word "mistake."

2. Ask each person to begin a round of free association (first person says "mistake" and each one in turn responds with one-word related answers).

3. Each person takes a turn beginning and ending one round of answers. Other words that can be used include: "error," "mishap," "wrong," and so on.

4. At the end of each round, ask everyone to complete this sentence: "To me being wrong means . . ."

5. Ask the group to outline a healthy attitude for "mistakes." Ask everyone if they are willing to let this be the attitude for their group.

Issues for Discussion

- Family of origin issues about making mistakes

- Feelings experienced when a mistake is made

Questions to Consider

1. What would you have to do to improve your attitude toward making mistakes?

2. Are you able to admit when you've made a mistake?

3. What have mistakes given you the opportunity to do?

Participant Affirmation

My mistakes are powerful teachers.

Leader Affirmation

My mistakes guide my learning.

Vignette 2

Goal: To expand the idea of mistakes and use them to grow

Example: A male group member had just finished a session with a female client who reported she had been raped. She walked in the session, he said, and hand delivered to the therapist her own solutions and plans to handle this situation. The therapist listened carefully, not interrupting. When he shared this case in group he described it as "textbook" in terms of finding exceptions, none of which he had to ask for. He felt he had done nothing and therefore had made a serious mistake.

Challenge: To honor his view of his "mistake" and use it to help him see the situation in another way.

Intervention: As the leader, I offered him this: "I can see where you feel you did nothing. It sounds as if this woman had reached her own answers and needed another person to hear this and support her conclusions about what she should do." He nodded that he had done this. "I wonder," I continued, "what it would have been like for her if you had interrupted her and told her what she must do." He responded: "I would have taken something from her." "Yes and in doing so, she could have felt raped again. Sometimes, doing nothing means you did all you could. Often that is much harder than doing something."

SFT Principle: Use what appears to be a mistake as a lesson. Honor the hard work of client and therapist.

Exercise 3: "My problems are my best friends." —Frank Lloyd Wright

This exercise teaches us that problems we face are really teachers, lessons, and friends. So we can begin to have the attitude that mistakes and problems are helpful. This also opens the door for dealing with "being stuck" in a therapy session. This encourages therapists to work out of "being stuck."

Time: 30 minutes

Materials: Pen and paper

Concept: Examine members' views of what it means to have a problem, and how views can help therapists who get "stuck" in a session

Directions

1. Ask members to fold a piece of paper in half.

2. On one side, ask them to complete this sentence, "Best friends do . . ." (or the question "What do best friends do?" can be used). Allow five minutes for them to complete this part.

3. Next ask them to turn the paper over and make a list under this heading, "Problems do . . ." (or the question "What do problems do?" can be used). Allow five minutes for them to complete this part.

4. Ask them to compare the two lists.

5. Members may read each of their lists aloud so that the group can compare their ideas.

6. Discuss reactions.

7. Ask each member to repeat another word for "problem." Do several rounds of this and ask the group to react to the words offered by the group.

Note: The usual responses include: "always there," "sensitizes you," "accepts you where you are," "there to help you," "never goes away." These reactions are readily seen as applicable for best friend and then for problems. This is usually a startling revelation.

Issues for Discussion

- How the view of "problems" affects therapy

- How the "problem" lists are similar to the "best friend" list

- Benefits of different views of "problem" to the therapist

Questions to Consider

1. What is different between a problem and a best friend?

2. Which is more constant?

3. How are these two similar?

Participant Affirmation

Problems I run into can be my guides. I can trust that their presence will help me learn.

Leader Affirmation

Problems can be my teachers if I choose to learn from them.

Vignette 3

Goal: To help group members understand how they view having problems and their feelings about having problems

Example: The group was asked to list the traits of a "best friend" and a "problem." Group members listed these phrases: "around me a lot," "won't leave me," "sticks by me no matter what," "something that I can learn from," "expected," and so on. They reached the conclusion that problems offered much the same things to each of us that our best friends are capable of offering.

Challenge: To keep the focus on "problem" and "best friend" until meanings for these words coincide.

Intervention: As the leader, I offered the challenge to the group to see the benefits of friends and problems. I said to the group: "Describe each word using short phrases to see what we come up with." I then waited till the meanings coincided.

SFT Principle: Seeing problems as challenges, using what the client brings or our own difficulties to teach us.

Exercise 4: See the System!

This exercise teaches the systematic principle of connectedness of all members of a system. It encourages each therapist to see his/her connection to each member of the client system. Therapists who practice from other models will like this exercise; they will be able to relate what they already do to the picture of a network or "spider web."

Time: 1 hour

Materials: Yarn in three different colors, scissors, case example

Concept: Portraying family as a system by using role-playing and yarn; three levels of communication are used: calm and congenial, slightly irritated, and highly agitated. Concepts of fusion, triads or triangles, stability, change, dyads, and interrelatedness are considered.

Directions

1. Select four or five participants to take part in a role-play.

2. Ask if they are willing to portray a family. Assign roles of father, mother, siblings, or any other roles in a family structure. This group selects a family problem to portray.

3. Give these instructions to the "family": "As you role-play, every time you speak, wrap the yarn around your finger and pass it to the person you are addressing or any person in the 'family' who responds. That person, in turn, wraps the yarn around their own finger as they speak and so on, until a network of yarn begins to form."

4. Three rounds of role-playing are completed to form three different modes of communication. Round 1: Use one color of yarn (such as blue) and have the family discuss an issue in a calm, routine manner. Leader should cut the yarn after about 5 minutes of conversation. Round 2: Leader starts the second round by offering the family the second color of yarn (such as yellow). The family discuss the same issues with a little more emotion. Have the family members tighten the yarn slightly as they develop the

network. Leader cuts the yarn again after 5 minutes of conversation. Round 3: Use a third color of yarn (such as red) to construct a network of family communication around the problem the family is having. The discussion this time should be heated and the red yarn should be tightened.

Issues for Discussion

- The network of yarn remains intact and forms the basis for discussion.

- Terms such as dyads, triads, triangles, enmeshment, distance, implied power, and system can be examined by looking at the yarn "web" or "network."

- It is helpful for group members to comment on aspects of what the "system" of yarn looks like, the role of each family member, action and reaction in the network, effect of loss of a member from the system, and anything else that comes to mind.

Questions to Consider

1. What would happen to this system if a member died? (This can be portrayed by having a member pull hard and then untangle from the network and asking each remaining member for reactions.)

2. What would happen if family members became very rigid about a particular issue? (This can be portrayed by having members pull and tug on the network and asking members for their reactions to this.)

3. If each family system can be viewed as a dance with each member having a step in the dance, then what does the therapist have to do to join with this family and other families? (This can be shown by having the whole network start moving until the group gets into a pattern and then having the leader try to join in without changing the motion of the family.)

Note: Another way to enhance this exercise is to ask the family members to move in some kind of rhythmic motion until they arrive at a distinct pattern, caused by all of them. Others not in the activity can discuss how to enter this family system and what a therapist would have to do to join their motion. Answers are usually about movement but can readily be translated into techniques from other therapy models or Okun's list of helpful behaviors. An alcoholic or drug addicted family can be portrayed by every member pulling on their strings at once and in an erratic manner.

Participant Affirmation

I can recognize the patterns of interaction in families and learn how to join with each one.

Leader Affirmation

I can join in the motion of this family without interrupting their pattern of interaction.

Vignette 4

Goal: To help group members have fun understanding the concept of a "system" and how members of a system interact and connect

Example: Every time I have done this exercise, participants see the connections in the string network. They see how they influence and are influenced by others and by the whole system.

Challenge: Keep this exercise flowing and inclusive of terms for therapy, such as "network," "web," "triangles," "influence," "closeness," "distance," and "scapegoat." I ask for conclusions about systems in general from any group. This exercise can be adapted to fit any kind of system, including alcoholic systems, work systems, etc.

Intervention: I simply ask for participants' observations and conclusions.

SFT Principle: Concept of system and interrelatedness of the members of a system.

3

There Am I: The Client's View

In this chapter, we really make an effort to see the world of a client from the client's point of view. We learn that the words others use to explain their dilemmas give us access to their view of their problems. We learn to listen for and use their "language." Goal setting, flexibility, and flowing with resistance are the issues of this chapter.

Exercise 1: Windows—Seeing Client Views

This is good practice for finding the "client's view." It helps the therapist listen to the exact words of the client and begin to use them. The therapist can also see the impact of using client words or refusing to use them. The impact can be seen in facial expressions of the clients and in how well they think they are understood.

Time: Overnight assignment or in-class assignment (30 minutes each)

Materials: None

Concept: Practice getting someone else's viewpoint and seeing things as they see them

Directions

1. Ask a volunteer to talk about a current dilemma in his/her life. Ask that the problem be a routine problem and not highly personal.

2. As the volunteer talks, members gather four unique phrases that the volunteer used to describe the problem and the volunteer's view of self.

3. Each member draws a window as shown below:

Phrase 1

Phrase 2   *Phrase 3*

Phrase 4

4. Assign the potent descriptors used by the volunteer to describe the problem to their proper positions on the window—most potent to number one position, next potent to number two position, and so on. Write out how the volunteer sees self in this situation. Use three words from the client's language to do this.

5. Each member, in turn, shares the potent descriptors with the volunteer. The volunteer then confirms whether each member has seen her/his view of the problem of her/himself.

6. Ask each member to talk about their feelings toward the volunteer.

Note: This exercise can be used with colleagues who are irritating. Example: If we find someone irritating and then we allow ourselves to see the world as s/he sees it, we are less inclined to find the person irritating.

Issues for Discussion

- What made it easy to get the descriptors

- Any distractions from collecting the potent phrases that members found

- Ways to honor views of colleagues who are different

Questions to Consider

1. What were the distractions that the members experienced in listening?

2. What is important about what distracted them?

3. What was the effect on the volunteer when she/he felt heard?

4. What are the basic skills in "good listening"?

5. The last time each member knew that someone really heard him/her, how did that feel? What did the listener do that made the volunteer know they were being heard?

Participant Affirmation

I can grow in the way that I listen to others. I can understand a very different way of looking at things.

Leader Affirmation

I can model good listening by the way I listen to others in my group.

Note: This exercise can also be a take-home assignment: Ask each member to listen to someone they encounter often in their daily lives and repeat this exercise, following the same steps as outlined above. Each person then shares the results with the entire group.

This can be repeated as often as necessary in order to get practice in the area of seeing another person's views. It is particularly helpful to ask members to select someone who sees things very differently than they do or who irritates them.

Vignette 1

Goal: To experience entering another's world through her/his words

Example: Hearing one group member's situation offered the chance to enter his world, one that happened to be very different, even from the world and world views of the group members. The instructions were to listen closely and record the prominent, emotionally charged phrases in his speech.

Challenge: To listen for the potent phrases, without being distracted and to use any distractions to aid the therapist's personal journey.

Intervention: As the group leader, I offered these words: "It is really fun to see if we can discover and keep up with what is important to Tom. If Tom is our client, it is our job to enter his world through the window he creates for us without disturbing what we find there. We can learn from what distracts us as well and use those distractions to understand ourselves as developing therapists."

SFT Principle: Listening for potent phrases that offer the therapist a window on the client's world, and recognizing and dealing with distractions.

Exercise 2: More Windows

This is more practice at hearing others and their feelings. This exercise really invites us into a practice of getting others' ideas about their situations and their feelings. We get to enter others' worlds and be a companion to them there.

Time: 30 minutes

Materials: None

Concept: Gain practice in seeing things the way others view them

Directions

1. Members pair off and each is asked to discuss a problem or concern.

2. One is designated as the listener and one is the client. The first client takes five minutes to explain a problem.

3. The listener records four potent phrases that the client uses to describe the problem and him/herself.

4. The listener shares these with the client and verifies that she/he accessed the "client view."

5. The client then shares how she/he feels about being heard.

6. Repeat the whole process, reversing roles.

Issues for Discussion

- The affective experience of being heard

- Possible effects on clients if they are not heard

- What the therapist does in terms of behavior to be fully present for the client

- Possible effect of getting the client view on the outcome of therapy

Questions to Consider

1. What does it mean to be fully present for someone else?

2. What does being "fully present" mean in behavioral terms?

3. What would some possible effects on the client be if the therapist chose to use client language throughout the therapy (or alternately therapist's language)?

Participant Affirmation

I honor others by listening to how they say things and recognizing their views.

Leader Affirmation

I am capable of seeing the views of others and I honor what I see.

Vignette 2

Goal: To help therapists in the group leave their worlds and enter the world of their clients in a respectful way

Example: The group was working on a case together. We worked as a team with one therapist in front of the mirror doing therapy and the rest of us were behind the mirror watching and working. The client expressed debilitating grief upon the death of her dog that afternoon. Some members of the group struggled with the idea of her grief being "debilitating."

Challenge: To honor their questions about this as well as the client's position of extreme grief.

Intervention: As the leader, I offered this to the team behind the mirror: "I understand that to some of you this kind of grief makes no sense. I comprehend this kind of grief myself, because I have felt it several times. What would it take from you to honor this client where she is right now?" Members stated that they would have to set aside their own feelings and listen for the potent, important words she used to describe her situation. I followed that with this question, "What kinds of things could you do with your own feelings?" Once each outlined what they had to do to join this client where she was, they could find the important phrases from this client and enter her world.

SFT Principle: Accept emotional reactions even if they do not make sense in our world views.

SKILLSHEET 2 Seeing Their Views—Exercises 1 and 2

Instruction: Hand out skillsheets before the group session begins.

	Not Evident	Needs Work	Good	Very Good
1. Follows client topic using questions	1	2	3	4
2. Uses client language	1	2	3	4
3. Asks questions to understand	1	2	3	4
4. Identifies and writes four phrases that sum up the client problem and view of self	1	2	3	4
5. Verifies client view with client	1	2	3	4
6. Client confirms that counselor understands view	1	2	3	4

Exercise 3: Metameaning

This exercise asks therapists to think about the premises of Solution-Focused Therapy in symbolic form. Again, this is getting out of the usual mode of thinking and into a symbolic, imaginary, fun approach to the same ideas.

Time: 2 hours

Materials: None

Concept: Use of metaphorical ideas

Directions

1. Ask members to visualize or recall a metaphorical example for each of the basic premises of SFT listed in Chapter 2 of the Manual.

2. Ask members to pair up and complete each of these phrases:

   a. Building on deficits is like:

   b. Listening carefully enough is like:

   c. A preconception is like:

   d. Waiting for awareness to happen so that one can change is like:

   e. Symptoms are like:

   f. Seeing change as an inevitable constant is like:

   g. A system is like:

   h. Small change leading to bigger change is like:

   i. Fixing what already works is like:

   j. Believing that complicated problems do not need complicated answers is like:

   k. An exception to a problem is like:

   l. Seeing a problem existing in a context of thoughts, feelings, and behaviors is like:

   m. A rule without exception is like:

   n. Problems occurring in patterns are like:

Issues for Discussion

• Premises listed above that give members concerns and the origins of these concerns

Questions to Consider

1. What ideas are easiest to accept?

2. What ideas challenge my current thinking?

3. Why? What does this say about me?

Participant Affirmation

It is thrilling to challenge my own ideas.

Leader Affirmation

Others challenge me and we both grow.

Vignette 3

Goal: To help group members think about concepts in a fun and symbolic way, building the idea that symbols help us to think about problems differently

Example: Having the group members go through each of the SFT premises is fun. There is usually a lot of laughter and the concepts are not then seen as so difficult. This is about the time when group members express frustration with one or more concept in SFT. This exercise, done in partners and then shared with the entire group is fun and helps each person to "try again."

Challenge: To keep this fun and then compare notes on the symbols selected for each principle.

Intervention: I offered this as group leader: "Let's look at all these frustrating new ideas in a slightly different way. Pick a symbol for each of these ideas and free associate whatever comes to mind."

SFT Principle: Working with whatever mood the group members bring, looking for a slightly different view of the concepts being learned.

Exercise 4: Joining Their Dance

This exercise teaches the principle of flexibility for the therapist and how to join the pattern of a client system. It also helps therapists to flow with the events of a session and be gentle with themselves as they do it. Therapists' feelings about doing this are often instructive of the next steps in the development.

Time: 30 minutes

Materials: String, cut in lengths about thirty inches long, one for each trio of group members

Concept: Finding and using the natural rhythm of a couple and joining that rhythm without disrupting it

Directions

1. Ask group members to divide themselves into trios.

2. Two group members play a couple and the third is the therapist.

3. Ask members playing the couple to tie themselves loosely together with the string. The third person leaves the room for a minute or two.

4. Ask that they move the string together as a pair in such a way as to form a rhythm.

5. The third person then returns to their assigned trio to study the pattern of movement between the partners.

6. The third person maneuvers to merge with the pattern of the couple and attempts to stay in sync with the couple for a few minutes.

7. Discuss with the group what it took for the therapist to merge in each couple.

Issues for Discussion

- Who needs to be flexible in a session

- What each therapist in each trio had to do to merge with each couple

- Requirements of each therapist (Usually, these answers are movements of some kind and the leader can then ask members what would be required in terms of behavior and counseling skills in order to merge with their assigned couple.)

Questions to Consider

1. What behaviors are necessary for each therapist in order to merge with each couple?

2. What role does flexibility play in a good therapy session?

3. What skills does each member think they need to improve?

Participant Affirmation

Each couple has a unique rhythm and I recognize and honor that rhythm. I can be with it without disrupting its flow.

Leader Affirmation

I study the rhythm I make with each group member. Each rhythm is unique and unfolds before me.

Vignette 4

Goal: To join the natural rhythm of a couple or a family system

Example: The previous exercise is expanded to see the patterns or rhythms that exist in couples and families. The therapist is asked to study how it can be done with "volunteer" clients and situations. Group members then list the behaviors that they used to join with the volunteer couple or family.

Challenge: Keep the focus on the various rhythms and the behaviors it takes for the therapist to merge with each couple or family.

Intervention: Amidst the usual laughter that goes along with this exercise, I ask these questions: "What did it take for you to join with your clients?" (Get a list of behaviors, thoughts, feelings.) "What do you think their response was to your efforts?"

SFT Principle: See a pattern in the interaction of couples and families and find ways to join with those patterns.

4

Setting a Goal for Therapy

In this chapter, we learn about goal-setting for both voluntary and involuntary clients, looking at strategies that help clients chart the courses of their therapy.

Exercise 1: What Has to Be Different?

This exercise is about goal-setting for voluntary and involuntary clients. This helps the therapist stay on track with goal-setting and help clients set reachable goals.

Time: 1 hour

Materials: None

Concept: Setting a goal

Directions

1. Members pair off with one as listener and the other as client.

2. The client begins to discuss a problem and the listener collects four potent phrases. The listener also asks these questions: For voluntary clients, "What has to be different as a result of coming to therapy?" For a client who doesn't want counseling, "What do you have to do differently so that you don't have to come for any more counseling?"

3. If the client answers in vague terms, the listener uses these follow-up questions: "What will you be doing differently when the problem is solved?" "Is this your goal for therapy?" "What is your goal for therapy?"

4. The listener wants a goal for therapy that can be measured. This can be a behavioral, cognitive, physiological, or affective goal as long as it can be measured.

5. After 10 minutes the listener shares his/her recording of the client views of the problem and self as well as the goal for therapy.

6. The client then assesses the work of the listener in getting the views and the goal and how it felt to be heard.

7. Repeat entire process, reversing roles.

Issues for Discussion

- Ways to make client goals measurable

- Staying on track with goal-setting

- Possible issues that may distract therapists from setting measurable goals for the therapy

Questions to Consider

1. If the client feels safe to express him/herself what does that mean for the therapy?

2. For all members: What would it take for you to feel safe as the client in therapy?

3. How does it feel to you when someone uses your words to describe something?

Participant Affirmation

When I validate others, I am validated myself.

Leader Affirmation

I make a place of safety for others when I honor their efforts and accept their views.

Vignette 1

Goal: Help group members find ways to help clients set goals

Example: Therapists learning the SFT method often miss the mark when helping a client set a goal for therapy. Goal-setting gets lost when searching for views, exceptions, and compliments. Therapists set aside the need for a goal that helps determine when the therapy is successful and when it is finished. They also give the client a goal rather than placing the client in the position of determining one. This is particularly true when the client has many problems or refuses to name just one, or does not want to be in therapy.

Challenge: To help group members ask good questions.

Intervention: I asked group members to use these questions as a starting point to help each client find a goal for therapy.

1. What has to happen so that you know therapy has been a success for you?

2. What will be changed in your situation?

3. What will be better when therapy is over?

For the client with many goals:

1. Which problem would you like to solve first?

2. What would you like to do with the other problems you have mentioned while we work on this one?

I also ask group members to list for themselves other questions that would help nail down a specific goal. I then ask them to ask themselves if this goal is in some way measurable, so that when success is reached, everyone will know.

SFT Principle: Helping the client choose a workable goal.

SKILLSHEET 3 Setting a Goal—Exercise 1

Instruction: Hand out skillsheet before group session begins.

	Not Evident	Needs Work	Good	Very Good
1. Uses client language	1	2	3	4
2. Pursues topic by use of questions	1	2	3	4
3. Gets four phrases that explain client view of problem and view of self	1	2	3	4
4. Asks goal questions	1	2	3	4
5. Gets specific goal by asking "What will be different in your life as a result of therapy?" and if appropriate—"When you are not doing that any longer, what will you be doing differently when the problem is solved?"	1	2	3	4
6. Gets measurable goal (list what will be different when the problem is solved)	1	2	3	4

Exercise 2: Understanding Resistance

This exercise prepares the therapist for the experience of resistance in therapy or the lack of resistance as demonstrated in SFT. We get the idea of what it is like to flow with what happens in the therapy room. We get the idea of what it is like to let go of our own agendas.

Time: 30 minutes

Materials: String, cut in lengths about 30 inches long

Concept: Using resistance and discussion of its effects

Directions

1. Ask everyone to pair off.

2. Ask one person in each pair to be the client and the other to be the therapist.

3. Hand out the string—one length for each pair of participants.

4. Partners attach the string to one of their hands and begin a tug-of-war with each other.

5. Let the tug-of-war continue in each pair for a minute or two. Then ask each pair to let the "client" partner win.

6. Stop the process and ask the group of "therapists" what their feelings are about this experience. Ask for one-word descriptions.

7. Ask the "clients" about what their feelings are about this experience. Ask for one-word descriptions.

8. List on the board the feelings of those who were the clients and those who were the therapists.

9. Repeat process with partners switching roles.

Issues for Discussion

- Issues of control in session

- What it feels like to let the client lead

- Outcomes of letting the client lead

- What happens when the therapist leads

Questions to Consider

1. Who is in charge of the session?

2. Who is in charge of changing?

3. Who is in charge of the rate at which a change takes place in the life of a client?

4. What benefits are there for therapists who let clients lead? Detriments?

Participant Affirmation

It is safe and healthy to let others lead their own lives.

Leader Affirmation

I can let others guide their own learning.

Vignette 2

Goal: To understand resistance as unknown patterns that can be known and cooperated with

Example: When group members experience resistance and cooperation with a piece of string, this is both fun and instructive. One important piece of the learning is understanding that systems have rhythms and that the therapist's job is to join each rhythm in a way that enhances what is going on in that rhythm. Participants understand what it means to "fight" with a client and to "go with the flow" presented by the client. They also have the chance to examine their own feelings about such issues as "control" and "change."

Challenge: Keep the focus on understanding rhythms and learning to merge with various rhythms.

Intervention: I ask these questions: "What were your feelings as therapist when you let go?" "What did it feel like when the therapist gave into your lead?" "What did you notice about the rhythm of your clients?"

SFT Principle: Going with the flow of each client.

5

Using Client Strengths

Client strengths are an essential factor in SFT. In this chapter we learn to listen to the clients, accept their view of their problem(s), and find the strengths in relation to their view of the problem. Acknowledging these strengths, these "teachable moments," is crucial for both the therapist and the client.

Exercise 1: A Teachable Moment

This exercise trains the therapist to listen for what is going well in the life of the client from the client's point of view. It also teaches therapists about using client words so that the compliments given by the therapist fit the client's own self-image and view of the problem at hand.

Time: 1 hour

Materials: Pen, paper, chalk, blackboard

Concept: Seeing what others think they do well and offering compliments they believe to be true about themselves

Directions: The whole group works together.

1. One person volunteers to discuss a problem.

2. The group listens and makes a list of phrases that characterize the volunteer's view of the problem and self. The group gets the "client's view."

3. The group listens for any evidence that the client is doing something on his/her own in order to change the problem.

4. Each member of the group then states four aspects of the client view and two to three compliments for the client.

5. Group members are asked to watch the reaction of the volunteer as these views are read and the compliments are offered.

6. Ask the volunteer how it felt to be approached by therapists this way.

Repeat entire exercise with a new partner for more practice. Switch to a highly controversial problem to give members a bigger challenge.

Issues for Discussion

- Look at the experience of recalling someone else's exact wording

- Discuss mood of client in reference to self and problem

Questions to Consider

1. How does it feel to have a therapist use your words?

2. What does it require of the client if the therapist does not use her/his words?

3. What possible meanings might a client derive from a therapy situation where the therapist uses her/his words right away?

4. What impact will using the client words and phrases have on cooperation in therapy?

Participant Affirmation

I listen to how others say what is important to them and use these words to discuss it with them.

Leader Affirmation

I listen to the words that are important to others and use these in conversation with them.

Vignette 1

Goal: Review of compliments and strengths gained in the previous exercises

Example: One group member offered a horror story as a problem. There was nothing good about her situation and no way out of it. Her situation as she told it got worse and worse and her view of it was terrible as well.

Challenge: Group members try to find client view and strengths.

Intervention: I said this to the group: "Her situation is really bad, so it is important to respect that and find within it something she will agree with that has brought her through it even a little bit."

SFT Principle: Accept the client's view regardless of what it is and find strength within that.

SKILLSHEET 4 Compliments—Exercise 1

Instruction: Skillsheets can be given to the group before the group session begins.

	Not Evident	Needs Work	Good	Very Good
1. Uses client language	1	2	3	4
2. Asks questions that pursue client topic	1	2	3	4
3. Asks goal questions	1	2	3	4
4. Helps client set specific goal	1	2	3	4
5. Gets four phrases that make up client view	1	2	3	4
6. Listens for client impact on problem	1	2	3	4
7. Names four client strengths that the client believes to be true about her/himself (using client language)	1	2	3	4
8. Lists compliments in client language	1	2	3	4

Exercise 2: Very Teachable Moments

This exercise further hones the therapist's ability to enter the world of the client and leave his/her own world for a time. This fine-tunes the therapist's ability to work with "difficult" clients and to learn at the same time what distracts therapists.

Time: 10 minutes

Materials: None

Concept: Practice listening to persons who have different opinions from the listener, and refusing to be distracted by attributes of others

Directions

1. Participants are asked to select someone in their lives to whom they find it difficult to listen. (This is a real challenge if the person that is difficult to listen to is also annoying to the listener.)

2. In routine conversation with this person, members agree to listen to their persons as the persons are routinely encountered.

3. Everyone is asked to list three views of their "difficult" person and three compliments that the "difficult" person would believe about him/herself.

4. Each person is asked to write down the views and the compliments and think about how their "difficult" person views the world. Each person is then asked to think about the compliments.

5. Each member is asked to share their feelings about their difficult person after completing this exercise.

Note: Feelings toward the difficult person usually change slightly—just enough to see the difficult person's point of view. The members usually report an improved understanding of the way the difficult person sees things as well. The challenge is also for members to discuss another person's point of view and set their own aside, using client words.

Issues for Discussion

- Changes that the members felt toward the difficult person after doing the exercise,

- What that process of change was like for each individual person

Questions to Consider

1. What is the impact of seeing another's different view on the therapy? on the therapist? on the client?

2. What does a therapist have to do to visit the world of someone very different from her/himself?

Participant Affirmation

A person who has very different views is someone from whom I can learn.

Leader Affirmation

Those who present different ideas enrich my understanding.

Vignette 2

Goal: Helping each other with distractions offered by clients and finding ways to stay in the worlds they present

Example: I ask our group members to find someone in their daily lives who irritates each one of them. They are to listen to this person and find four phrases in their words that are potent descriptors of their world views. Each member is also to look at what usually distracts him/her from understanding the irritating person's point of view. Each member lists the distractions and shares them with the group. When we have done this exercise, we have found that group members' opinions of the irritating people have changed a little bit, toward a more understanding and civil position.

Challenge: Keep the focus on the four potent phrases, understanding personal distractions and how these affect therapy, and working with others we do not like.

Intervention: I asked these questions: "List the four potent phrases that give a window to the world of your irritating person." "What distracted you and why?" "What did you have to do to get back on track?" "What do your distractions say about you?" (I ask that group members work on this one privately.) "What can you do with these distractions in your own life?"

SFT Principle: Get a difficult client's cooperation by listening to what is important to him/her.

6

Looking for Strength:
The Search for Exceptions

In this chapter, we practice listening for exceptions, times when the problem somehow differed. We learn to apply this thinking personally and to stay focused on the exceptions in relation to the goal for therapy. This leads to the final element in the intervention formula, the homework task.

Exercise 1: Hearing the Exceptions

This exercise helps the therapist listen for times when others describe exceptions to their own situations. It also teaches the therapist to make use of these times in the search for exceptions in the therapy session.

Time: 30 minutes

Materials: None

Concept: Listening for exceptions

Directions

1. Ask the group members to pair off.

2. One person will discuss a problem while the partner listens.

3. The partner should listen in the conversation for words that indicate the problem varies somehow.

4. The partner lists the words that indicate a degree a variation, such as "usually," "sometimes," and so on.

5. Partners switch roles and repeat the process.

Issues for Discussion

- Effect on therapy of focusing on times when the problem varies

- Effects on therapy of focusing on the nature of the problem only

Questions to Consider

1. What is the experience of the clients when they hear that the therapist is interested in times when the problem varies?

2. What are the possible effects on the client when the focus is on how the problem varies?

Participant Affirmation

Problems vary in severity; I can train myself to hear differences in everyday speech.

Leader Affirmation

I can see that problems vary; I can help group members to see these variations.

Vignette 1

Goal: Finding conditions in everyday talk that indicate an exception or variance in the condition.

Example: I asked a group member to offer a pretend problem to the group. He was asked to begin talking about it. The group was asked to listen for times when the problem varied and how it varied, or exceptions. Within five minutes, there had been three.

Challenge: Help therapists listen for, recognize, and use variance (exceptions) as these arise naturally in the client's conversation.

Intervention: I asked group members to list all the words or phrases they could recall that indicate a variance in condition of something, such as, "almost," "every now and then," "sometimes," and so on.

SFT Principle: Search for times when any problem varies.

SKILLSHEET 5 Hearing Exceptions—Exercise 1

Instruction: Before the group session begins, hand out the skillsheets.

	Not Evident	Needs Work	Good	Very Good
1. Gets four phrases making up client view	1	2	3	4
2. Lists three compliments client believes to be true about him/herself	1	2	3	4
a. Lists exception words in client conversation	1	2	3	4
b. Asks individual exception questions	1	2	3	4
3. Asks relationship exception questions	1	2	3	4
4. Balances relationship exception questions among partners or family members	1	2	3	4
5. For every "when" question, counselor asks "What did you do that helped?" and "How was that better?"	1	2	3	4
6. When client gives only one exception, counselor asks, "What else?" many times	1	2	3	4
7. Uses client words in forming exception questions	1	2	3	4
8. Determines number and type of exceptions client has	1	2	3	4
9. Determines type of task to use (spontaneous, deliberate, or combination)	1	2	3	4

Exercise 2: My Own Exceptions

This exercise helps the therapist to see exceptions in her/his own life and see hope for themselves by doing so. They can also see what has helped them thus far and figure out what to do next.

Time: 30 minutes, outside class

Materials: Paper, pencil

Concept: Thinking about how my own problems vary in severity

Directions

1. Ask group members to consider a problem they are having.

2. Ask each to select a goal that is measurable.

3. Ask each to list times when the problem was a little bit better. (A list of four or more is really helpful.)

4. Ask each person to write down on that list what they were doing differently at the time that the problem was different.

5. Ask that each one determine what kind of exceptions were generated from asking these questions.

Issues for Discussion

- Effects on therapy and on client when these questions are used

- Effects on client and on therapy when they are not used

Questions to Consider

1. What was your immediate reaction to the questions in this exercise?

2. What was your internal process in relation to the problem?

Participant Affirmation

I have a strength within me to solve my own difficulties. Solving them is a process under my direction.

Leader Affirmation

I can solve any dilemma I am having when I trust that my own wisdom leads my process.

Vignette 2

Goal: To help group members see that their own problems vary and in this variance they may find strength

Example: When group members look at their own problems and ask themselves exception questions, a remarkable thing usually happens. They often become more hopeful. They find renewed strength and an increased sense of mastery over their own situations. It is helpful for them to experience what inevitably their clients will feel in therapy done this way.

Challenge: Keep everyone focused on their own issues and the search for strength. Writing down their exceptions helps them lock into their strength, so that it is very clear to them.

Intervention: I use these words with group members: "Let's see if there is any value in buying for ourselves what we say we want to sell to our clients. What exceptions did you find in your own behavior? What compliments would you give yourself? What do you need to do next in your situation?"

SFT Principle: Find our own exceptions and personal strength so that we can understand the situation of clients doing the same thing.

Exercise 3: Asking Exception Questions

This exercise helps the therapist to stay focused on exception questions related to the client's goal for therapy. This is something that must be practiced often. The therapist gets practice in wording exceptions and finding many times when the problem was different.

Time: 1 hour

Materials: None

Concept: Wording exception questions to fit with client ideas

Directions

1. Ask members to pair off with someone they do not know very well in the group.

2. One partner begins to tell a problem and the other listens. (This problem should not be one of critical importance in the life of the person offering it; rather, it should be fairly simple and straightforward. The point here is to get practice asking exception questions in an interview style format and look at concerns that come up for students in this process. The goal is not to do therapy.)

3. The partner listens for views and compliments and asks this string of questions a number of times:

   "When was this problem better?"

   "What did you do to get it that way?"

   "How did that help?"

4. The partner lists the views, compliments, and exceptions, sharing these with the "client."

5. The partners switch roles and repeat this process.

Note: Encourage participants to let their partners tell their stories and weave these questions in the conversation at points that seem to be appropriate times. Participants should also be encouraged to "borrow" the wording for these questions from the language used by their "clients." Ask each "therapist" to keep their notes from this experience.

Issues for Discussion

- Effect on members who played the client

- Problems in finding a balance between the telling of the client story and the interweaving of the questions

Questions to Consider

1. What are the challenges of approaching an interview this way?

2. Just from these interviews, what might be the benefits of therapy done this way?

3. What is the reaction of each group member to exception questions? Do the questions sound mechanical or do they sound like part of the conversation?

Participant Affirmation

My questions and my problems guide my learning.

Leader Affirmation

Questions enrich the learning experience. I am comfortable with answers I know and leave the rest for another day.

Vignette 3

Goal: Practice interviewing using exception questions that are woven into the conversation

Example: We listened to one group member talk about a problem he had with finances. He said he had had it for years, and that he felt he was irresponsible. He said he wanted to be more responsible but was unsure what that would look like in his life. He said he had alienated his wife with his "irresponsibility."

Challenge: To ask exception questions in relation to a specific goal set by the client.

Intervention: I offer these questions to the group members as a guide: "What has to change for you?" "When was this situation any better?" "When it was better, what did you do?"

SFT Principle: Having the client set a goal and search for strength as the client tries to reach it.

7

Interventions

In this chapter we begin to write interventions, and we see how the parts come together to form a message for the client. We look at what we believe about strength and weakness and how that affects the therapy we do.

Exercise 1: Writing an Intervention

The therapist collects information for all the parts of the intervention and gets real practice at writing an intervention. The therapist gets practice using the stated format so that it begins to form a way of thinking about therapy and client problems. This format also helps to show the therapist the parts of SFT that still need more work.

Time: 30 minutes, in class or outside class

Materials: Paper, pen

Concept: Writing an intervention from the ideas collected in the previous exercise

Directions

1. Ask members to reread Chapter 7 in the Manual.

2. Using the information collected from Chapter 6 interviews, ask them to write an intervention in the format given on page 69 of the Manual.

3. Ask each member to present the client situation using the case presentation format in the book and then read the intervention aloud for each partner who played the role of the client.

4. Group members watch the reaction of each partner (both verbal and nonverbal).

5. The group then discusses how well each intervention fit. Each discussion about fit is led by the partner whose problem the intervention addresses.

Issues for Discussion

- Problems that came up in trying to find exceptions

- Problems with weaving everything together to form a comprehensive intervention

- Ways to resolve those problems

Questions to Consider

1. What differences do group members feel (if any) toward the problem they are facing after the interview?

2. What is the reaction of each member to the hearing of questions? Do the questions sound mechanical or do they sound like part of the conversation?

3. Did the intervention help them see their problem in a more positive light?

Participant Affirmation

I can get the information I need to write a good intervention. The fit need not be perfect; it need only be good enough.

Leader Affirmation

I hear all questions as guides to the learning process.

Vignette 1

Goal: Writing an intervention using the formula

Example: After group members had collected information from the volunteer client, they reviewed the client view, (four potent phrases), compliments that the client would accept as true, and the number and type of exceptions. Using the formula in the Manual, they each wrote their own intervention. Concerns that arose were how to begin the intervention and the rationale for the same, choosing the proper words, and so on.

Challenge: To keep the focus on writing the parts of the formula and reminding group members to determine number and type of exceptions.

Intervention: I asked these questions: "What are the potent phrases that were vital to this client's story?" "What are some strengths that the client will agree with?" "Name the goal for therapy." "What are the exceptions that this client listed?" "What kinds of exceptions were there?" "What kind of intervention matches these exceptions?"

SFT Principle: Accept client strengths and build on them, set a goal for therapy, use compliments, and find exceptions.

SKILLSHEET 6 Writing Interventions—Exercises 1, 2, 3

Instruction: Hand out to group members before the group session begins.

	Not Evident	Needs Work	Good	Very Good
1. Counselor uses client language	1	2	3	4
2. Lists client views in client language	1	2	3	4
3. Lists client compliments	1	2	3	4
4. Lists client exceptions	1	2	3	4
5. Specifies number and type of exceptions	1	2	3	4
6. Specifies type of task to use	1	2	3	4
7. Writes intervention in client language and in paragraph form, using format from the Manual	1	2	3	4

Intervention = Client View + Compliments + Homework Task from Exceptions

	Not Evident	Needs Work	Good	Very Good
8. Reads intervention to client	1	2	3	4
9. Checks to see if client agrees with task	1	2	3	4

Exercise 2: Hearing Strength in Others' Problems

This exercise looks at the difference when problems are viewed as challenges or severe deficits. Group members can get feedback on how this feels from a volunteer "client." Group members have more opportunity to practice hearing the views of others and showing respect for others' views.

Time: 1 hour, outside class

Materials: Pen, paper, friend with problem

Concept: More practice in interviewing

Directions

1. Ask members to find a friend who will allow them to practice this style of interviewing with them.

2. Ask members to repeat the process used in the previous exercise.

3. Ask members to ask their friends what the process felt like to them.

4. Have everyone make a list of their friends' reactions.

5. Ask them to discuss these reactions in the group.

Issues for Discussion

• How interviewees felt at the end of the interviews

• Any new insights interviewees had as a result of the process

• Surprises that members experienced in the process

Questions to Consider

1. What would be the difference in the interview if the conversation had centered on problems and how bad these are?

2. What does the view chosen tell each member about his/her own goals?

Participant Affirmation

Listening for others' strengths in problem situations helps me to develop my skills in listening.

Leader Affirmation

Cooperation is enhanced when I listen for and accept the views of others.

Vignette 2

Goal: To practice interviewing and writing interventions

Example: In one of the pairs of group members, no exceptions were found. The volunteer client had reported no change and no coping mechanisms. This stumped the therapist and opened the discussion for understanding that the interview questions are themselves interventions and do not have to be answered when asked. The questions have staying power beyond session time.

Challenge: The challenge here became the study of therapists wanting things to go a certain way and at their pace. We could look at the effect on therapy of their subtle push for change.

Intervention: Group members were frustrated with no apparent way out of the current client situation. I offered this "way out": "We can find a way out (their words) by letting the client lead in his own time and in his own way. If we hurry him, he may decide that he cannot trust or work with us."

SFT Principle: Accept views that are different. Get on board at the client's pace.

Exercise 3: Practice, Practice, Practice!

This exercise helps the therapist get more practice in interviewing, hearing the client views and writing interventions. Each part of the intervention can be discerned and interventions can be practiced. There is also the chance for therapists to learn a balance in using questions and letting clients tell their stories.

Time: 1 hour for each of the next several meetings

Materials: Pen, paper, case examples, audio, or video equipment

Concept: Getting practice in interviewing, listening to the client story, and writing interventions

Directions

1. Ask members to bring in case examples on video or audio tapes to share with the class.

2. The job of the members is to determine if a clear goal for the therapy has been established. If not, what happened? The group lists strategies to get the goal narrowed to a workable objective. If there is more than one client, there should be a measurable goal for each.

3. The second task is to listen for client views and compliments for *each* client in the session.

4. The third task is to listen for and list the exceptions. Each person determines the number and type of exceptions in each interview.

5. Each person writes an intervention and class members read these aloud to compare them.

Issues for Discussion

- Challenges in balancing the focus between hearing the clients' stories and asking questions

- Improving wording of questions (Improvement means using client words)

- Asking questions that are focused in a solution direction and related to the goal

- Using the clients' language as part of the questions

Questions to Consider

1. What has to change in me so that I can ask better questions?

2. What assumptions do I have about therapy or clients that hinder the work I am trying to do at the present time?

3. What assumptions do I have that help me?

Participant Affirmation

It is safe and enlightening to make mistakes.

Leader Affirmation

When I model comfort with my own mistakes, others relax with their own work.

Vignette 3

Goal: To look at the effects of practice on the delivery of therapy

Example: Each participant brought in tapes of sessions that showed different problems in learning the model. One showed a dilemma in setting a goal, and several others found the potent phrases hard to find. Several asked exception questions about everything, not in relation to the stated goal for therapy. The group members were very frustrated.

Challenge: Accept where group members are and encourage them, find something good in the work they did.

Intervention: I reviewed the strengths shown in the work of each group member. I gave out compliments that fit and cast the next steps for each of them as "challenges."

SFT Principle: Accept that there is strength everywhere, find some of it, and use it to set the stage for the next steps.

8

Paths to Solution:
Structure of Sessions

In this chapter, there is more chance to see mistakes as lessons, by watching and discussing a leader's tape of a therapy session.

Exercise 1: One Example

This exercise is exciting because the therapists are asked to critique a supervising clinician. This gives that clinician a superb chance to take the one-down position and learn from others. If the supervising clinician has made mistakes in a session, then other therapists can see that mistakes can be lived through and can be "lessons."

Time: 1½ hours

Materials: Pen, paper, audio or video equipment, case example from leader's caseload

Concept: Leader presents a case to the group and asks for a critique of the work

Directions

1. Leader presents case using case presentation format from the Manual. (It helps everyone if the case presented is very relevant to their needs or touches concerns they have.)

2. The members view a video presentation of the leader's case. Their assignment is to collect the usual information and write an intervention.

3. They are also asked to stop the tape at any time they have questions.

4. Finally, they are to critique the performance of the leader using these phrases: "What I thought you did well ..." "What I think there needs to be more of ..."

Issues for Discussion

- The value of viewing others' work as having components of strength and challenges

- Others' views of "mistakes"

- The value of studying mistakes

Questions to Consider

1. What is learned from success?

2. What is learned from mistakes?

3. How are goals affected by each?

Participant Affirmation

I learn from my mistakes as well as my successes.

Leader Affirmation

Mistakes and successes are great teachers.

Vignette 1

Goal: To give group members more opportunity to review a case and to write and accept interventions

Example: I brought a suicide case in for the group to review. I asked the group for help with the case and especially to find questions that could have been worded in a more powerful way. (Dealing with serious problems such as suicide was a real concern for my group.)

Challenge: To encourage input from the group members and wait for them to word the questions.

Intervention: I gave this instruction: "I would like for you to critique this case, find errors in questions that I used and reword them. You may stop the tape at any time. Also list your ethical concerns as you would approach a case with this type of problem."

SFT Principle: Use apparent mistakes to help learning and growth.

Exercise 2: Writing a Case Presentation

Often therapists work with other colleagues who use a different model of therapy. This exercise prepares therapists to discuss their cases with colleagues of all points of view.

Time: 30 minutes, in class or outside class

Materials: Information gathered in previous exercise

Concept: Practice using the case presentation format in order to discuss sessions with colleagues

Directions

1. Ask students to refer to case presentation format on page 82 of the Manual.

2. Using the information they gathered in the previous exercise, have each person write a case presentation.

3. Discuss the outcomes and the benefits of writing these case presentations.

Issues for Discussion

- Working with colleagues who use different styles of therapy

- Not forcing one's method of therapy on colleagues

Questions to Consider

1. How can I work with colleagues who don't use my method of therapy?

2. Must I set aside my own ideas to understand their ideas?

3. How can I share my ideas in a non-offensive way?

Participant Affirmation

I can work with therapists who don't share my ideas or methods.

Leader Affirmation

The client, not my ideas, is the most important part of therapy.

Vignette 2

Goal: To practice working with others who do not share our views of therapy

Example: A colleague once told me that he was convinced that his current way of doing therapy was "correct." I refused to challenge him. I noted aloud to him the positives of his model. At the same time I let go of the need to convince him my way worked too.

Challenge: Letting go of the need to persuade others to do therapy the way I do it.

Intervention: I simply said this: "Wow, that sounds like it really works for you." I thought to myself: "My way works too, there are many ways to work."

SFT Principle: Accepting a view that is different from mine, while refusing to argue, compete, or persuade.

Exercise 3: Talking in Metaphors

This helps therapists to see where they are in their growth and development in a fun and playful way. If they get too caught up in their emotions around learning, they have the chance to be lighthearted and outline their next steps. If this is done in a nonjudgmental manner, it really is a lot of fun. Staying in the language of the metaphor also helps challenge the therapist's ability to identify and assume a client's view and language.

Time: 1 to 1½ hours

Materials: None

Concept: Catching up with metaphors and development of therapists from the beginning of group

Directions

1. Ask each person to talk about how his/her metaphor has changed or is changing. (Use language that fits the metaphor, for example, if someone is a turtle, then change might be described as "slow and steady.")

2. Everyone listens and comments on strengths emerging in each person (staying with the metaphor presented by each person).

3. Leader follows participant comments with a question to each one about future development.

Issues for Discussion

- Whatever issues come up in the discussion

Questions to Consider

1. What challenges have participants already met?

2. What are the next challenges for each one?

3. What compliments would each person give him/her self?

Participant Affirmation

I set and meet my own challenges at a pace that is right for me.

Leader Affirmation

I set the right pace for myself as an instructor; as I learn and grow, so do those around me.

Vignette 3

Goal: Review development of group members as therapists through the symbols they chose

Example: Group members talked about their stages of development in terms of each particular symbol, such as a turtle or butterfly. Each member spoke in terms related to the specific object or chosen symbol, describing growth in those terms as well. Group members supported each other with compliments.

Challenge: The challenge here is to keep each person talking in terms of the selected metaphor.

Intervention: When each group member spoke of his/her symbol I asked questions in terms that also described the symbol selected. With the turtle symbol I asked about her pace, her "hard shell" she had described earlier, and so on. With the butterfly, we asked about flight patterns and knowing which flowers to land on, and so on. This conversation was still in line with each person's goals as a developing therapist.

SFT Principle: Accepting where each person is and taking note of strengths in symbolic terms.

9

Strength Undefeatable:
Scaling Questions

In this chapter, we learn to expect strength and to look for it where there appears to be none. We use scaling questions to measure improvement before, during, and near the end of therapy for individuals, couples, and families.

Exercise 1: Seeing Invisible Strength

This exercise teaches the use of scaling questions to help find strength where there appears to be none. It also gives therapists the chance to use client words in these questions, to find compliments (see things upside down), and to let go of how things "should" happen for the client. This exercise teaches therapists to stay out of the way and let clients "do their own things." Therapists learn to "accompany," not direct.

   Time: 10 minutes for each question

   Materials: None

   Concept: Marking success numerically using scaling questions

Directions

1. Participants pair off and one begins to tell the other a problem. The counselor in this exercise will ask the following questions in the course of conversation:

   a. "On a scale of one to ten, with ten being the highest you could go and one being the lowest, where would you put yourself today?"

b. "In comparison to the time before you made this appointment, where would you put yourself on that same scale?" (improvement before sessions)

c. "If the 'client' has moved up on the scale in resolving the problem, how would the client explain this? What was done to move up?" (improvement during therapy)

d. "If the 'client' has gone down on the scale, then how does the client explain that it is not any lower on the scale?" (still searching for strength in the worst situations or relapse)

e. "If the 'client' is far from the goal, what number must be reached in order for the client to consider therapy a success? What must the client do in order to move it up one number? All the way to the goal number?" (outlining the work to be done)

2. Ask everyone to discuss their experience of these questions with the entire group.

3. Repeat the same process switching roles.

Note: Remind members to use client language in wording of their questions.

Issues for Discussion

- Compliments that can be given to clients no matter where clients find themselves on the scale

- Use of the client language in asking scaling questions

- Have members scale their understanding of this model of therapy at the beginning of class and now

- The goal number (what number is "success?")

- The steps left to reach their goals

Questions to Consider

1. What does it mean to clients if the therapist continues to search for strength?

2. What kind of experience might the client have if he/she is asked to discuss improvements?

Participant Affirmation

As I reach for my goals, I am watching for signs of my success.

Leader Affirmation

As I reach for my own goals, I am aware of my own success. I enjoy others' success as well.

Vignette 1

Goal: Use scaling questions to mark success with clients

Example: Group members played clients and therapists as before. They listened for about 15 minutes or just long enough to learn the client view, get compliments that fit, and find exceptions. Some were assigned to scale improvement in the problem before the client began to discuss it, during their conversation, in the life of the client, and in setting the goal each client sought and how close they were right now to that goal. Each pair found that scaling questions shed different light on the problem at hand. To all, situations began to look hopeful.

Challenge: Help participants ask scaling questions that are related to the goal for therapy.

Intervention: I offered this to the group: "Remember to ask scaling questions to find out how close your client is to his/her goal or how much work is yet to be done. Once you have an idea of the numbers that a client reports, you can help them specify the next step, the number that will represent success to the client and the work that is left to be done. "

SFT Principle: It is easier to build on success than it is to build on deficits or weaknesses.

Exercise 2: Scaling Questions with More Than One Client

This exercise teaches the use of scaling questions with more than one person or "relational scaling questions." Relational questions are key in SFT, as this exercise teaches. Therapists get to see healing take place in a context of relationship. They further have the opportunity to see strength in relationship and see couples and families work out their own solutions.

Time: 1 hour

Materials: Video or audio case examples

Concept: Using relational questions to find improvement in couples and families

Directions

1. Using video or audio case examples with couples or families, members write and discuss as a group examples of scaling questions that are relational in nature.

2. Discuss how these questions focus the therapy on solutions and client goals.

3. Discuss how these questions form a matrix or context for healing.

Issues for Discussion

- How context promotes healing

- How relational healing and individual healing take place in context

- Examination of the resources in a couple/family that promotes healing

Questions to Consider

1. What techniques do members use to help them focus on the couple's strengths?

2. What strategies can therapists use to get themselves back on track when they find themselves off track with couples and families?

3. What distracted the listeners from using scaling questions?

Participant Affirmation

I can learn something from getting off track with couples and families. I can devise my own strategies to get back on track.

Leader Affirmation

I can help other therapists understand what helps them to stay on track and how to get back on track in their work with couples and families.

Vignette 2

Goal: To construct good relational scaling questions

Example: Participants often struggle with the construction of relational scaling questions. They often ask one person of a couple in therapy and overlook the need to balance their questions by asking the same question of the other partner. The same situation occurs when therapists meet with families. Therapists are really asking information about the "system" when relational questions are used. In one instance, group members were practicing asking relational scaling questions and several clients reported "being overlooked."

Challenge: Help participants see the connection between persons in a relationship and to ask questions about the changes that need to be made in that relationship. Also, therapists need to be reminded to ask these questions in relation to the stated goal for therapy. Many things in therapy can be scaled such as success toward a goal, hope, trust, the work left to be done, achievement, and the average level of acceptable success in the mind of the client.

Intervention: I offered some examples of relational scaling questions:

A husband and wife wanting to recover from alcoholism and its effects:

To Wife: On a scale of one to ten with ten being high and one being low, where would you put your hope that Sam will stop drinking? (individual scaling question)

To Husband: Sam, where would you put yourself on that same scale? (individual scaling question)

To Husband: Sam, what would you guess it would take for your wife to move that score up to where you think it is? (relational scaling question)

With the group, we then think out loud about a case and construct many scaling questions, both relational and individual, and discuss the differences and how to use them in sequence related to a specific goal for therapy. A video or audiotaped case example is helpful here.

SFT Principle: Look at strengths and build on them. See members of a system as related and affecting other members of that same system.

SKILLSHEET 7 Marking Improvement with Scaling Questions— Exercises 1 and 2

Instruction: Hand out before group session begins.

	Not Evident	Needs Work	Good	Very Good
1. Uses client language	1	2	3	4
2. Gets specific goal	1	2	3	4
3. Gets client view	1	2	3	4
4. Uses individual exception questions	1	2	3	4
5. Uses relationship exception questions	1	2	3	4
6. Gets list of exceptions	1	2	3	4
7. Determines number, type of exceptions	1	2	3	4
8. Determines type of task	1	2	3	4
9. Asks scaling questions in relation to therapy goal	1	2	3	4

*Scaling self today   1————————————————10

*Scaling before appointment was made   1————————————————10

*Scaling any progress   1————————————————10

*Scaling relapse   1————————————————10

*Scaling closeness to goal   1————————————————10

*Scaling next step   1————————————————10

	Not Evident	Needs Work	Good	Very Good
10. Asks what behaviors are next to meet goal for therapy	1	2	3	4
11. Uses scaling questions that are relational with each member of couple or family	1	2	3	4
12. Balances scaling questions with partners, among family members	1	2	3	4

10

Worst-Case Scenarios: Just Getting By

In this chapter, we learn to look for strength in the worst of human situations.

Exercise 1: One of the Worst Times in My Life

This exercise helps therapists enter the worst situations to see the view of the client and leave their own ideas at the door of the therapy room. Therapists can see that persons, including themselves, really do cope. They can remember personal coping and strength and it is hoped from that position the therapist can "let" the client struggle and cope. The therapist can identify preconceived notions about really awful situations and discuss how these ideas hinder therapy.

Time: 15 minutes outside group; 30 minutes inside group session

Materials: None

Concept: Finding strength in tough situations

Directions

Part One

1. Ask members to think about a specific time when things were rough; ask them to list what they did to cope with the situation.

2. Ask them what strengths were derived from this tough situation.

3. Ask them to list their assumptions about humans and their coping mechanisms (a list of about four to five sentences).

Part Two

1. Ask participants to remember the hardest time in their lives; ask that they list the most helpful thing they did to get through the situation. Ask that they describe to themselves how this helped them. Ask that they list all the things they can think of that helped at that time.

2. Ask that they consider what kept them from giving up entirely. Ask how this helped.

3. Ask group members to list their assumptions about humans and coping abilities in the toughest of human situations.

Issues for Discussion

• Ask members to share something from their lists that they are comfortable sharing with the entire group

Questions to Consider

1. What happens to human strength in the worst of human situations?

2. What are the usual mechanisms that humans use to cope?

3. What kinds of coping mechanisms make group members uncomfortable?

4. What is the value of seeing some kinds of coping mechanisms as "pathological"?

Participant Affirmation

The ways I cope may not be the ways others cope; everyone has unique coping mechanisms.

Leader Affirmation

I watch the ways others cope and realize everyone, including me, has unique approaches to solve problems.

Vignette 1

Goal: Look at coping through horrible situations

Example: Each member was asked to describe a very difficult time to the others in the group. Each was asked to pick a problem that they had worked on quite a bit. Really dire situations that participants had not confronted were not used. Each member listed his/her coping mechanisms and then each was asked to prioritize their abilities to cope. A list of personal strengths was produced by each. Then assumptions about "tough" times were discussed by the group members. After reviewing their own abilities to cope, it was difficult to see clients as lacking strength in even the worst of situations.

Challenge: Keep everyone focused on finding ways that they coped with their situations.

Intervention: I offered this to the group: "Be sure to figure out what helped you through, even if you did nothing different. See if doing nothing helped. Figure out how you kept going."

SFT Principle: Finding strength in the hardest of times, seeing others as strong.

SKILLSHEET 8 Dealing With the Worst Times—Exercise 1

Instruction: Hand out skillsheet before group session begins.

	Not Evident	Needs Work	Good	Very Good
1. Counselor names a "worst" time for him/her	1	2	3	4
2. Lists personal strengths that helped	1	2	3	4
3. Lists what she/he did that got her/him through situation	1	2	3	4
4. Lists strengths gained from worst situation	1	2	3	4
5. Lists behaviors of others that were helpful to him/her at that time	1	2	3	4
6. Lists unhelpful behaviors of others at that time	1	2	3	4

Exercise 2: Writing Interventions for the Worst of Human Situations

This exercise helps the therapist use all the SFT skills learned to write useful interventions for the worst of human situations. This exercise offers the therapist the chance to let the client do the struggling. The therapist can accompany and look for strength.

Time: 1 to 1½ hours for each situation

Materials: Pen, paper, case examples

Concept: Practice in writing interventions with a team

Directions

Part One

1. Two members volunteer to role-play. They leave the group and decide on a worst-case scenario for the group.

2. They return to the group and the one who is the counselor interviews the other who is the client.

3. With the rest of the group listening and collecting the usual information, the counselor does a complete interview keeping in mind the guidelines for using "coping" questions from page 102 of the Manual.

4. The rest of the group serves as a team and at 45 minutes after the hour, the counselor takes a break from the client and meets separately with the team.

5. Together, under the direction of the counselor, they write the intervention.

6. The counselor and the team return to the client and the counselor reads the intervention to the client.

7. The client gives immediate feedback to the counselor and the team regarding how well the intervention fit.

Part Two

Repeat for another type of tough situation with more than one person as a client.

Issues for Discussion

- Assumptions that get in the way of looking for solutions

- Personal issues that come up for therapists as they deal with tough situations

- Ways to deal with personal issues that come up for the therapist during a session

Questions to Consider

1. What does it mean for the therapist when his/her own issues come to the foreground when dealing with a client in a therapy session?

2. What are some options for dealing with issues that come up for the therapist in sessions with clients?

3. What are group members' ideas about therapists going into therapy?

Participant Affirmation

When my personal issues emerge in a therapy session, I take note of this and work out a plan for myself after the session.

Leader Affirmation

When my personal issues come up as I lead the group, I see this as normal and take care of them elsewhere.

Vignette 2

Goal: Putting together interventions for the hardest times

Example: When we discussed the difficult times that some of us had experienced, group members were easily distracted, probably because they were taken aback by what they heard, how others' pain matched their own, or what they had not worked through. This is often the case with new therapists and their clients. They can't hear anything but their own agenda when their own unresolved problems resemble those of their clients. They often get lost in what they are hearing.

Challenge: Separate client goals from the distractions and advice offered by group members, and keep everyone searching for strength.

Intervention: I offered this to the group: "List what pulls on you emotionally while each of us is talking. See what idea about the problem being discussed emerges from this 'emotional pull.' Also list what problems were easier for you to hear and begin the search for exceptions."

SFT Principle: Find the client view and stay within that. Search for client strength, finding our own agendas that may hinder this search.

SKILLSHEET 9 Interventions for the Worst of Times—Exercise 2

Instruction: Hand out before the group session begins.

	Not Evident	Needs Work	Good	Very Good
1. Uses client language	1	2	3	4
2. Gets client view	1	2	3	4
3. Gets specific goal	1	2	3	4
4. Considers coping as a goal	1	2	3	4
5. Uses worst-case questions	1	2	3	4
6. Uses coping questions	1	2	3	4
7. Uses exception questions	1	2	3	4
8. Uses appropriate scaling questions	1	2	3	4

	Not Evident	Needs Work	Good	Very Good
9. Uses self-talk if necessary	1	2	3	4
10. Writes intervention using formula	1	2	3	4
11. Takes note of distractions and makes plan to solve	1	2	3	4

Intervention = Client View + Compliments + Task from Exceptions

11

Crises and Urgent Problems

In this chapter, we look at the kinds of ideas the therapist may have and how these hinder or help the therapy. Issues that offer detours and sidetracks for the therapist in the therapy hour are discussed also.

Exercise 1: The Truth About Crises

This exercise asks the therapist to look at her/his personal views of crisis situations. Therapists can discuss the benefits of a flexible belief system on clients, problems, and therapy.

Time: 1 hour per problem situation

Materials: None

Concept: Studying common beliefs about very serious problems

Directions

1. As a group, members list their beliefs about each of the problems discussed in Chapter 11 in the Manual.

2. The group then discusses the effects of these beliefs on hope for change, the therapy itself, and the client experiencing the problem.

3. The group then lists alternate ways of looking at these problems that free the therapy to go where it needs to go.

Issues for Discussion

- How beliefs the therapist holds dear affect therapy

- What is the power of belief

- What it takes to change one's belief about anything

Questions to Consider

1. How does the client benefit from a therapist with a flexible belief system?

2. How does the therapist benefit by being flexible in her/his belief system?

Participant Affirmation

I can change my beliefs or keep them and study their effect on the therapy I do.

Leader Affirmation

I can help others to examine the effects of their beliefs on therapy. I can examine the effects of my own beliefs on the way I work with others.

Vignette 1

Goal: To get at what we believe about very serious problems and how our beliefs influence therapy

Example: Group members discussed the meaning of the word "crisis." We also asked about each others' reactions to specific crises and listed ones that we thought had the power to distract us from our work as therapists. Each list differed a little bit and each member explained why a particular crisis event had the power to distract.

Challenge: Keep the focus on the power of the nature of crisis and our emotional reactions to each one.

Intervention: I offered this to group members: "The character for crisis in Mandarin Chinese brings together two characters, one representing danger and the other representing opportunity. Let's see the danger and opportunity in each crisis we examine. Let's also see the impact viewing danger and/or opportunity will have on the therapy we do."

SFT Principle: See strength even when things are at a crisis point.

Exercise 2: Assumptions About Therapy with Chronic Problems

Therapists can look at their assumptions about therapy with chronic problems and the various paces that clients use to heal. This gives therapists a chance to examine different paces and paths that clients take on their roads to healing.

Time: 1 hour

Materials: Video case examples

Concept: Studying assumptions of how to work with chronic problems, and finding the pace at which healing proceeds

Directions

1. Using audio or video case examples or case reports, members present their work with clients who have chronic problems. The group studies the pace of the client and how well the therapist is matching the pace.

2. The group stops the video and discusses the assumptions behind the processes of healing in chronic problems.

3. The group then examines the effects of their assumptions on the outcome of the healing process and the process of therapy.

Note: Members should use the Case Presentation Format found on page 82 in the Manual when discussing each case. This will help the group to stay focused on the process of solutions.

Issues for Discussion

- Ways to stay focused on solutions

- Problems that arise in trying to stay focused on questions

- Finding a balance between hearing the client's story and asking solution questions

Questions to Consider

1. What assumptions do the group members have about chronic problems that help the therapy process?

2. Which assumptions about chronic problems hinder the process of therapy?

3. In reference to assumptions that hinder, what are these assumptions really about for each group member?

Participant Affirmation

I can alter my assumptions as I see the need and watch the impact of this change on the therapy I do.

Leader Affirmation

I can alter my assumptions to help myself and others.

Vignette 2

Goal: Studying our assumptions about clients with chronic problems

Example: The group reviewed a number of cases with clients who had chronic problems. As the tapes of these cases were played, members of the group wrote down their assumptions about each type of problem. As a group, we looked at how our assumptions can impact therapy and lead to certain outcomes.

Challenge: Keep the focus on assumptions and where they lead.

Intervention: I offered this to the group: "What do we learn about ourselves when we study our own assumptions about an issue or client problem? What do our assumptions tell us about our past and how we do therapy now? What limits do I place on myself, the client, and therapy with these assumptions?"

SFT Principle: Review therapists' assumptions about client problems that can hinder the therapy.

Exercise 3: What Did the Client Really Mean?

This exercise offers the therapist the chance to identify the issues that sidetrack him/her in the therapy session. Therapists can then figure out what their "sidetracks" say about them or steps they need to take to deal with "sidetracks."

Time: 1 hour discussion

Materials: Case examples

Concept: Making sure the therapist understands the meaning the client intended, using what client brings to therapy

Directions

1. Members discuss the importance of understanding idiosyncratic phrases used by clients.

2. Members discuss the value of using these questions in therapy:

- "What does this (dream, thought, feeling, event) mean to you?"

- "How is this (dream, thought, feeling, event) related to what we are working on?

3. Members discuss how these two questions can help to keep the client focused on the stated goal of therapy.

Issues for Discussion

- Use of the two questions above with clients who have a litany of complaints or who do not seem to be moving toward solution

Questions to Consider

1. What kinds of issues are sidetracks for me as a therapist?

2. What does this say about me?

3. What do I need to do about the sidetracking issues I face?

Participant Affirmation

If I get sidetracked by client discussion, I can get back on track again. I can benefit by knowing what derails conversations from the path of solutions.

Leader Affirmation

I can understand the meanings that others give to the events in their lives. Doing this affirms them and improves my skills as a listener.

Vignette 3

Goal: Examining idiosyncratic responses of clients

Example: We reviewed several cases with clients who had used specific phrases that were vital to their descriptions of the problem at hand. These descriptions seemed emotionally charged and were very colorful. We outlined questions to get at the specific meaning to the client in each sequence we examined.

Challenge: Finding a meaning that was deeply personal to the client so that the therapist would have a clear understanding of the problem at hand.

Intervention: I offered this to the group: "As each of you presents your work, please show us the sequence where these emotionally charged and confusing phrases exist in the session you did with your client. We will stop the tape and offer different ways to ask the client to explain what she/he means in the words chosen."

SFT Principle: Get the client's real meaning.

12

The Twenty-Minute Interview

This chapter looks at what can be done with clients when there is only a short time for a session. Specific questions are outlined and practiced; they can be used with clients as well as with those who have referred them.

Exercise 1: Really Brief Therapy

This exercise offers practice in doing the twenty-minute interview and ways to stay on track in doing this interview. Therapists can look at ways to use the time they have, and the benefits of very brief therapy.

Time: 1 hour

Materials: None

Concept: Practice doing the twenty-minute interview

Directions

1. Ask members to pair off with each other.

2. One member will offer a problem from his/her own caseload and another will use the twenty-minute interview format with this problem. Basic guidelines and questions for the twenty-minute interview can be found on pages 132–133 in the Manual.

3. The member who is the therapist in this exercise should write an intervention as outlined in Chapter 7 of the Manual.

4. Members then switch roles and repeat the process.

Issues for Discussion

- Problems in doing the interview

- Ways to stay on track with the questions

- Ways to stay on track within twenty minutes

Questions to Consider

1. What possible benefits are there for doing therapy in a specified time frame?

2. What possible benefits are there for doing therapy in such a brief format?

3. What are the possible applications of a twenty-minute interview to other settings?

Note: The leader can suggest applying this method to a personal dilemma and see how it works to help members solve their own difficulties.

Participant Affirmation

I am capable of helping others find their own strength within a short time period.

Leader Affirmation

I am capable of helping others find their strengths using both the short and long interview formats.

Vignette 1

Goal: Learning and doing a short interview

Example: Again we worked in pairs and practiced the twenty-minute interview. Each pair used 3″ x 5″ cards with the stated questions in front of them. Partners found it easier to get back on track when using these cards. They recorded their interviews and then shared them with the group for encouragement.

Challenge: Keep partners on track with the questions and make sure that they find a list of exceptions rather than just one or two.

Intervention: I offered this to the group: "See what method works for you to help you remember the questions. Pay attention to what in the client's story gets you off track and what you did to get back on track."

SFT Principle: Trust group members to find the way that works for them.

SKILLSHEET 10 The Twenty-Minute Interview—Exercise 1

Instruction: Hand out skillsheets before group session begins.

	Not Evident	Needs Work	Good	Very Good
1. Identifies if client is voluntary or involuntary	1	2	3	4
2. Accepts client view	1	2	3	4
3. Uses client language	1	2	3	4
4. Uses these questions	1	2	3	4

- What has to be different as a result of you talking with me?

- When was the last time you did this even a little better than now? (ask several times)

- What were you doing differently at that time? (ask several times)

- On a scale of one to ten with ten being very sure and one being not sure at all, how sure are you that you could do some of the things that helped you, if you really wanted to?

- On that same scale, how likely is it that you will do some of the things that helped you again soon?

5. Uses involuntary question to start interview if needed	1	2	3	4

- What does _____ say has to be different so that you don't have to come here anymore?

6. Writes intervention using formula and in client language	1	2	3	4

Intervention = Client View + Client Compliments + Task (from Exceptions)

Exercise 2: Audio or Video Work for Practice

This exercise offers more practice and home review of the twenty-minute interview. This exercise helps therapists figure out their own tools to improve how they do with the brief form of SFT.

Time: 30 minutes for each participant, time as needed for each person to review at home

Materials: Audio or video equipment, quiet room

Concept: Practice on the twenty-minute interview and home review

Directions

1. The group members work together to make a video to use as a study guide. To do this, each pair will record their work on a single video. Copies can be made of this video or the original can be shared as a study tool for everyone to use at home.

Issues for Discussion

- Location for taping

- Logistics of setting up times for taping

- Use of the resource after the video has been made

Questions to Consider

1. What forms of study tools can be made to help the group follow the model better?

2. What ways are participants using to remember the interview format?

Note: If there is no audio or video equipment, role-playing with the group serving as a consulting team may be substituted.

Participant Affirmation

I can find the study tools I need to help me remember techniques and skills of this model.

Leader Affirmation

I am aware of the study tools I need to help me teach this model. I am aware of ways each of us teaches her/himself and I honor each of these ways.

Vignette 2

Goal: Getting practice in videotaping and critiquing others' work in a supportive way

Example: Group members practiced sessions and wrote interventions using videotape equipment and the twenty-minute interview. The group then came together to share their sessions and offer feedback to one another. The assigned task of the group was to find strengths and challenges in the work of each person and to find a supportive way to offer these comments. Participants were noticeably nervous about sharing in this way. I stopped tapes and asked for reactions to well-posed questions.

Challenge: Keep the focus on sharing each others' work in a positive and nonthreatening way, a way that supports the work each is doing.

Intervention: I used responses that I thought would encourage all members of the group. I offered these as examples: "What I really like that you did was . . ." and "what I wish you would do more of . . ."

SFT Principle: Find strength in all we do and mark the work that is left to be done in a positive way.

SKILLSHEET 11 Working with the Referring Person—Exercise 2

Instruction: Hand out skillsheet before group session begins.

	Not Evident	Needs Work	Good	Very Good
1. Listens to story from referring person and explains that his/her help is still needed	1	2	3	4
2. Acknowledges their hard work	1	2	3	4
3. Accepts their views	1	2	3	4
4. Checks client's story with referring person	1	2	3	4

5. Asks these questions:

   - What is the smallest change you can accept from (_client_)?

   - When was the last time you found her/him doing a little better on this?

   - What was she/he doing differently at that time?

   - What do you think you were doing that might have helped her/him be more like you want her/him to be? What else?

   - On a scale of one to ten, how willing are you to try some of these helpful things that you tried before?

6. Offers compliments for past hard work	1	2	3	4
7. Reassigns what has worked	1	2	3	4
8. Thanks referring person for help given to client and to counselor	1	2	3	4
9. Logs contact in client file	1	2	3	4

Exercise 3: Talking with the Referring Person

This exercise helps therapists make use of their phone time with referral agents. It offers the chance to see the referral agent as a part of the client system that must be treated. Therapists can examine their assumptions about the referral agent and how these assumptions help or hurt therapy.

Time: 20 minutes

Materials: None

Concept: Learning Part B of the twenty-minute interview: working with the referral agent

Directions

1. Members pair off and work together in a quiet place.

2. Each person takes his/her turn role-playing as the therapist or referring person.

3. Others play Part B of the twenty-minute interview.

4. Those who play the roles of the therapist collect views of the referring person, compliments, and exceptions. A request for continued help from referring person is made.

5. Partners switch roles and repeat process.

Issues for Discussion

- Difficulties in doing the interview

- Ways others stayed on track with the questions

- Ways to accept view of referring person

Questions to Consider

1. What assumptions do members have about the referring person?

2. What effect do these assumptions have on this brief intervention?

3. What are the strategies that members use to find compliments for the referring person?

Participant Affirmation

I can find strength in others who do not see their own strength.

Leader Affirmation

I can focus on strength in places where there seems to be none. I can help others do the same.

Vignette 3

Goal: Learning to use SFT techniques in short phone conversations with referring source

Example: Partners paired up to do mock phone conversations with each other as the referral agent. Problems selected came from previous exercises so that therapists could connect both parts of the twenty-minute interview format. Views, compliments, and exceptions were sought from each referral agent. In some cases, the referring person was new to the case so that only views and compliments were found. In other cases, views, compliments, and exceptions were found.

Challenge: Writing interventions without complete information and keeping focused on the questions of Part B.

Intervention: I offered this to the group: "Please keep in mind that some referral agents will be new to your case. You simply ask them to keep track of anything they do that helps their client do better. When we do get the three types of information, we can proceed as usual to write the intervention. The intervention should be spoken in as short a sentence as possible over the phone to the referral agent. The key, like always, is to get their views and offer compliments that fit, before asking them to do anything that helps their client."

SFT Principle: Build on strengths found in the context of the problem to help solve the problem.

Exercise 4: Very Brief Work!

This exercise teaches the therapist to do really brief crisis work using two questions. Therapists also can figure out what kinds of situations call for this brief intervention.

Time: 5–10 minutes

Materials: None

Concept: Using only two questions when there is a crisis or very little time

Directions

1. Group members pair off and select a crisis situation on which to focus. Members could be working on a Crisis Call-In Service and use these questions as well.

2. Those who play the therapists ask those persons in crisis these two questions:

   • When things were going better for you, what were you doing differently?

   • What is the first thing you need to do now?

3. Together, they draw up a list of exceptions. Then, these are reassigned.

4. Members switch roles and repeat the process.

Issues for Discussion

- Problems in using only two questions

- Adding another question

Questions to Consider

1. What is the value of these two questions in a crisis or time-limited situation?

2. What are some situations where this approach would be useful?

Participant Affirmation

I can make a small contribution in a crisis situation and this can make a difference. How I view a problem in therapy does make a difference in how the therapy progresses.

Leader Affirmation

A crisis, even my own, is both a danger and an opportunity.

Vignette 4

Goal: Using two questions to help in a crisis.

Example: Group members selected a crisis situation to discuss with one another. Each person was asked to be client or therapist and to discuss a crisis situation of his/her choosing. Two questions were used from the SFT model to begin to solve the problem.

Challenge: Help group members focus on the meaning of "crises" and what distracts them in each case.

Intervention: I offered this to the group: "See what the two short questions offered can do to change the problem. What happened to the client? What happened to the therapist? What happened to the problem?"

SFT Principle: Accept that clients have strength in the worst of situations, and that they can draw out a little strength if asked solution-focused questions.

13

Applications to Other Settings

In this chapter, we take a look at the application of SFT to other helping situations. We check in on the growth and development of each therapist as well.

Exercise 1: Applications to Other Settings

This exercise offers the chance for therapists to see how SFT in both formats can be applied to all kinds of helping situations. They get the chance to think philosophically and practically about how to apply the model to other settings for both involuntary and voluntary clients.

Time: 1 hour in group, 1 hour at home

Materials: None

Concept: Group members learn to focus on applying this style of therapy to other settings

Directions

1. Members discuss and list places where the twenty-minute and fifty-minute interview formats might be useful. Members should be encouraged to think about their particular interest areas or places where they currently work.

2. Members assign themselves an interest area and write five useful solution-focused questions that are relevant to their work situations. Members can imagine a case scenario and work from that.

3. These questions are then tried in these settings and/or read aloud to the group for discussion and refinement.

4. Each set of questions includes a goal question, exception questions, and scaling questions that assess hope for change and motivation to change.

5. Repeat this process for the involuntary client in each of these settings.

6. Repeat this process for situations with more than one client.

Note: Members may make another video to share as a study tool.

Issues for Discussion

- Using the views of clients to help them

- What it takes on the part of therapists to honor different client views

- Why this is sometimes hard to do

- In their settings, what happens in therapy when the therapist does not do this

Questions to Consider

1. In general, what is the view of the involuntary client?

2. How can this view be honored and used to help this type of client?

3. What does the therapist have to do to honor this type of client?

Participant Affirmation

I can devise the tools I need to meet clients where they are.

Leader Affirmation

I devise ways to work effectively with others. I see and acknowledge their ability to grow.

Vignette 1

Goal: Applying both interview formats to other settings

Example: As a group, we discussed where we thought these two interview formats would be helpful and how we would modify or add to them based on the needs of the setting. Members role-played sample questions they came up with for each of these settings.

Challenge: Keeping the focus on the needs of a particular context, and the questions relevant to the problems found in each context.

Intervention: I offered this to group members: "Select an example of interview questions from the text that more or less fits where you work. Then choose a client from your situation and role-play with another group member that problem. See how the questions you came up with fit or needed refinement."

SFT Principle: Use what works, change what does not, trust yourself and others to find what works.

Exercise 2: What Happened to the Metaphor?

This exercise further tracks the development of therapists from their metaphors. Therapists can enjoy tracking where they started, the trip they took, and where they are now. They can also determine their next steps. This exercise can best be done in the mood of celebration.

Time: 1–2 hours

Materials: Participant papers

Concept: Tracking the development of therapists

Directions

1. Members are invited to read their short papers to the group. They may also simply explain the stage of development where they find themselves. If they have written other works, such as poetry, they may read these as well.

2. Others listen and offer comments, recognizing the strengths of their peers. The discussion is particularly helpful if kept in the language of each person's metaphor.

3. Members get a chance to hear what they have done well.

4. The members complete the exercise by offering compliments to the Leader. (The Leader may have used a metaphor as well to trace his/her own development; this is a good time to share that information with the group.)

5. This may be the final session with the group. It helps to find closure by asking everyone to discuss what the entire learning experience has been like for them.

6. Take a final moment to figure out everyone's next step, as guided by each person's metaphor. For example, if turtle was the symbol, then the question is "What would turtle tell you is your next step?"

Issues for Discussion

- Skills that have improved for each person

- Outlining goals for their next steps in growth, ways to maintain success

Questions to Consider

1. What have I learned in this process?

2. What is the rationale behind the statement, "Clients are the best teachers"?

3. Two years from now, when I look back on my own progress what will I notice is better about my own style of doing therapy?

4. Two years from now, when I look back on my own progress what will my clients say about how I have improved as a therapist?

Participant and Leader Affirmation

I can examine my own strengths and enjoy what I do well. I can outline my next goals and the steps I need to take to get there.

Vignette 2

Goal: Seeing the accomplishments of members of the group

Example: This was always fun. Group members shared their own growth as therapists through their chosen metaphors, and offered feedback to others based on their chosen metaphors. Members shared short stories, even poems, about their development. In doing so, they outlined the steps they had taken (logical, left-brain approach) and symbolically described their journeys (right-brain approach). This was an uplifting experience. Each member shared his/her own strengths and outlined the next challenges in terms of the symbols chosen.

Challenge: Keep members discussing themselves in terms of their chosen metaphors, especially as relates to the future. Keep them focused on tracing their journey as a commitment to good practice.

Intervention: I offered the example of my own metaphor to the group: "I have started as a turtle, with a slow and measured pace, head coming out of my shell only to smell danger, and not seeing any, returned to my own business inside my shell, letting others do their own thing at their own pace" ... and so on....

SFT Principle: See and respect the pace of others.

Other New Harbinger Self-Help Titles

Flying Without Fear, $12.95
Kid Cooperation: How to Stop Yelling, Nagging & Pleading and Get Kids to Cooperate, $12.95
The Stop Smoking Workbook: Your Guide to Healthy Quitting, $17.95
Conquering Carpal Tunnel Syndrome and Other Repetitive Strain Injuries, $17.95
The Tao of Conversation, $12.95
Wellness at Work: Building Resilience for Job Stress, $14.95
What Your Doctor Can't Tell You About Cosmetic Surgery, $13.95
An End of Panic: Breakthrough Techniques for Overcoming Panic Disorder, $17.95
On the Clients Path: A Manual for the Practice of Solution-Focused Therapy, $39.95
Living Without Procrastination: How to Stop Postponing Your Life, $12.95
Goodbye Mother, Hello Woman: Reweaving the Daughter Mother Relationship, $14.95
Letting Go of Anger: The 10 Most Common Anger Styles and What to Do About Them, $12.95
Messages: The Communication Skills Workbook, Second Edition, $13.95
Coping With Chronic Fatigue Syndrome: Nine Things You Can Do, $12.95
The Anxiety & Phobia Workbook, Second Edition, $15.95
Thueson's Guide to Over-The Counter Drugs, $13.95
Natural Women's Health: A Guide to Healthy Living for Women of Any Age, $13.95
I'd Rather Be Married: Finding Your Future Spouse, $13.95
The Relaxation & Stress Reduction Workbook, Fourth Edition, $17.95
Living Without Depression & Manic Depression: A Workbook for Maintaining Mood Stability, $17.95
Belonging: A Guide to Overcoming Loneliness, $13.95
Coping With Schizophrenia: A Guide For Families, $13.95
Visualization for Change, Second Edition, $13.95
Postpartum Survival Guide, $13.95
Angry All The Time: An Emergency Guide to Anger Control, $12.95
Couple Skills: Making Your Relationship Work, $13.95
Handbook of Clinical Psychopharmacology for Therapists, $39.95
The Warrior's Journey Home: Healing Men, Healing the Planet, $13.95
Weight Loss Through Persistence, $13.95
Post-Traumatic Stress Disorder: A Complete Treatment Guide, $39.95
Stepfamily Realities: How to Overcome Difficulties and Have a Happy Family, $13.95
Leaving the Fold: A Guide for Former Fundamentalists and Others Leaving Their Religion, $13.95
Father-Son Healing: An Adult Son's Guide, $12.95
The Chemotherapy Survival Guide, $11.95
Your Family/Your Self: How to Analyze Your Family System, $12.95
Being a Man: A Guide to the New Masculinity, $12.95
The Deadly Diet, Second Edition: Recovering from Anorexia & Bulimia, $13.95
Last Touch: Preparing for a Parent's Death, $11.95
Consuming Passions: Help for Compulsive Shoppers, $11.95
Self-Esteem, Second Edition, $13.95
Depression & Anxiety Management: An audio tape for managing emotional problems, $11.95
I Can't Get Over It, A Handbook for Trauma Survivors, $13.95
Concerned Intervention, When Your Loved One Won't Quit Alcohol or Drugs, $11.95
Redefining Mr. Right, $11.95
Dying of Embarrassment: Help for Social Anxiety and Social Phobia, $12.95
The Depression Workbook: Living With Depression and Manic Depression, $14.95
Risk-Taking for Personal Growth: A Step-by-Step Workbook, $14.95
The Marriage Bed: Renewing Love, Friendship, Trust, and Romance, $11.95
Focal Group Psychotherapy: For Mental Health Professionals, $44.95
Hot Water Therapy: Save Your Back, Neck & Shoulders in 10 Minutes a Day $11.95
Prisoners of Belief: Exposing & Changing Beliefs that Control Your Life, $10.95
Be Sick Well: A Healthy Approach to Chronic Illness, $11.95
Men & Grief: A Guide for Men Surviving the Death of a Loved One., $12.95
When the Bough Breaks: A Helping Guide for Parents of Sexually Abused Childern, $11.95
Love Addiction: A Guide to Emotional Independence, $12.95
When Once Is Not Enough: Help for Obsessive Compulsives, $13.95
The New Three Minute Meditator, $12.95
Getting to Sleep, $12.95
Beyond Grief: A Guide for Recovering from the Death of a Loved One, $13.95
Thoughts & Feelings: The Art of Cognitive Stress Intervention, $13.95
Leader's Guide to the Relaxation & Stress Reduction Workbook, Fourth Edition, $19.95
The Divorce Book, $11.95
Hypnosis for Change: A Manual of Proven Techniques, 2nd Edition, $13.95
The Chronic Pain Control Workbook, $14.95
When Anger Hurts, $13.95
Free of the Shadows: Recovering from Sexual Violence, $12.95
Lifetime Weight Control, $11.95
Love and Renewal: A Couple's Guide to Commitment, $13.95

Call **toll free, 1-800-748-6273**, to order. Have your Visa or Mastercard number ready. Or send a check for the titles you want to New Harbinger Publications, Inc., 5674 Shattuck Avenue, Oakland, CA 94609. Include $3.80 for the first book and 75¢ for each additional book, to cover shipping and handling. (California residents please include appropriate sales tax.) Allow four to six weeks for delivery.

Prices subject to change without notice.